I CAN'T BELIEVE I'M *lace knitting*

MW01156276

Say the words "lace knitting" and the images that come to mind may be of the Victorian era, Shetland shawls, thin knitting needles and even thinner yarn. But lace knitting is so much more! Use *any* weight yarn and any size needles to create a beautiful, up-to-date design for today. Learn about charts and chart reading, tools that make lace knitting easier, stitches, helpful hints, and techniques. Try the Bookmark project just to see how easy knitting lace is, and before you know it, you too will be able to say "I Can't Believe I'm Lace Knitting!"

MEET *kay meadors*

"My passion is knitting," designer Kay Meadors says, "especially knitting lace."

Kay's affection for the art shows in her exquisite work. Several years ago, we were lucky to have Kay join us at Leisure Arts as an instruction writer while her husband, Michael, attended college. Once you know a little more about Kay's many creative talents, you wonder how she can possibly choose a favorite.

"These days, my hobbies include spinning and quilting," says Kay. "And I love weaving! I've got so many looms now that I had to set up a 'loom room.' But it's knitting I come back to every time. I have three lace shawls in progress right now. I can't seem to stop."

Kay's work as a designer and pattern tester was a perfect fit while she home-schooled her son. "I was able to work at home while Ben did school work. Recently, Ben helped me set up my blog, Natural State Knitter. Now, he's just started college, so I'm looking forward to beginning a new chapter in my life."

Whatever Kay chooses to do, you can be sure she won't be giving up her love of creating beautiful things. "When I close my eyes, I see new designs," she says. "It's endless, and it's wonderful."

To find more of Kay Meadors' excellent knit and crochet designs, visit www.LeisureArts.com.

LEISURE ARTS, INC.
Little Rock, Arkansas

KNITTING tools

First, let's take a look at what you'll need for lace knitting. Some tools are necessary and some tools that just make lace knitting easier.

KNITTING NEEDLES

Knitting needles are your most important set of tools in lace knitting. Some of the projects in this book call for double pointed needles **and** circular needles, some call for straight needles. It's highly recommended that you use knitting needles made of plastic, resin or bamboo when knitting lace. These materials are lightweight and tend to be less slick than metal, an asset when knitting with soft, thin yarn. Pay special attention to the needle points. Well-tapered points will be of immeasurable value. Also, check the joining between each needle point and the cable cord on your circular needles. Make sure there is a smooth transition to lessen the chance of snagging your yarn.

MARKERS

You'll need many types of markers for the projects in this book—round ones, coil or spring-shaped ones, and split ones. At times, you'll need to use all the different kinds, so it's a good idea to have all the varieties on hand. The round ones will be used to divide a round into smaller sections of stitches, so you'll need more of these than any other type of marker. Use the coil or spring-shaped markers to mark the beginning of rounds. These come in a variety of colors and are perfect for when a different color or type marker is needed to mark the beginning of a round. The split type markers are great for marking the beginning of a round when working on double pointed needles. Where the other markers could slip off the point, a split ring marker can be attached to the first stitch. You can also use scrap pieces of yarn tied around the needle as markers.

POINT PROTECTORS

These are just what the name implies; they protect the points of the needles. They slip on, keeping the points safe and your knitting from slipping off the needles. In some patterns, you'll be instructed to slip a point protector on one point of a circular needle while you are working an edging with the other point and a spare needle.

ROW COUNTERS

You'll be knitting patterns that have row repeats (lots of row repeats!). Purchase a row counter that can be set down on a table or a lap, or one that slips on the cable of a circular needle. While they're not automatic, counters are a big help in keeping track of the rows you have knit.

GAUGE RULER

A gauge ruler is placed on your piece so you can count the stitches and the rows to check what gauge you are knitting (*see Gauge, page 73*). It also has a row of holes that you can insert unmarked needles (such as double points or circulars) through to determine their size.

OTHER HELPS

Magnetic boards or a magnetic row finder, such as those sold for counted cross-stitch, can also be used for keeping track of the rows on a knitting chart. You can copy the chart at 200% and use the magnetic strip to mark your row, moving it after each row is completed. Memo notes can be used in the same way; simply stick one above and one below the row you're working to help you stay on track.

Blocking wires and rust-proof T-pins can make all the difference in what your lace looks like after it is completed (*see Wire Blocking, page 7*).

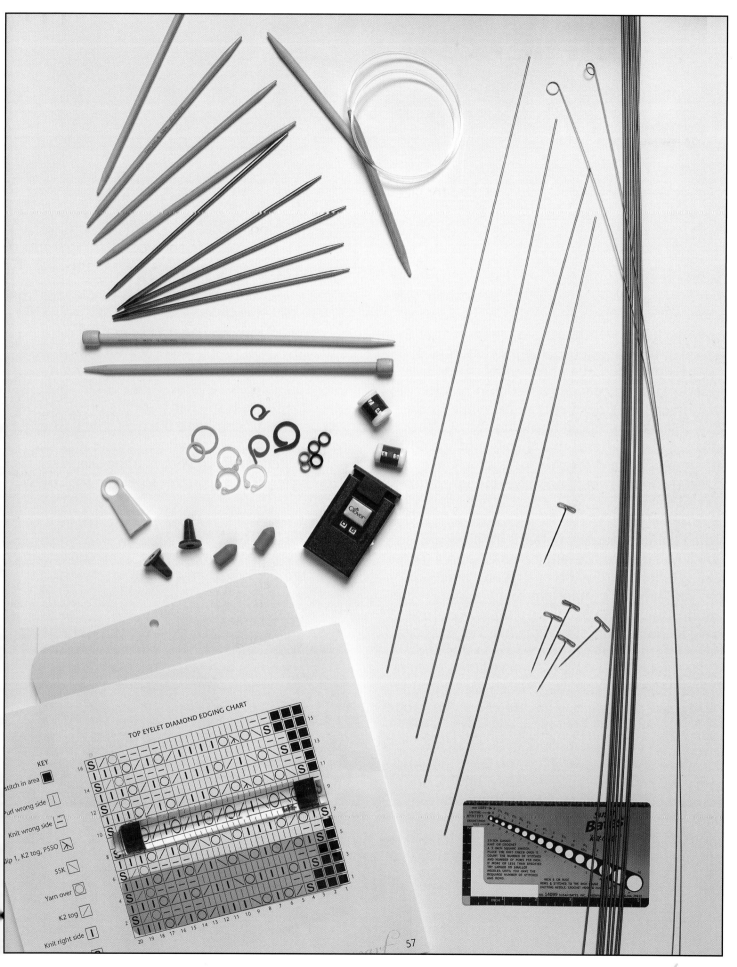

KEY

■ stitch in area

□ Purl wrong side

— Knit wrong side

☒ Slip 1, K2 tog, PSSO

◹ SSK

○ Yarn over

⟋ K2 tog

□ Knit right side

REFERENCE *guide*

Before beginning your first project, the Bookmark on page 9, take a moment to learn a little more about the basics of lace knitting, including reading charts, correcting mistakes and finishing.

GAUGE

You may ask, "Why is gauge so important in lace knitting?" One reason is the size of the finished projects. If you knit the Pillows and don't get the gauge in the instructions, the purchased pillows will be either too large or too small to fit inside. In some projects, gauge really doesn't matter all that much. The Bookmark can be a little smaller or a little larger without changing the overall effect. But, in patterns that specify a gauge and an amount of yarn/thread, not getting the gauge could mean that you'll not have enough yarn/ thread to finish.

When knitting the lace patterns in this book, you'll be asked to use larger needles and a gauge that is different from the one recommended on the yarn label. It's important that you obtain the gauge listed in the pattern. To do so, you may have to change the size of the needles you use. Before starting any of the projects in this book, it's absolutely necessary for you to knit a swatch in the stitch and with your chosen yarn and the needle size suggested. If you don't get the gauge with those needles, change needle sizes to get gauge. Go up in size if your gauge swatch is too small and go down if it is too large. Because everyone knits differently—loosely, tightly, or somewhere in between—the finished size can vary even when the knitters use the very same pattern, yarn, and needles. So take the time to do a proper gauge swatch; you'll be happy that you did!

CHARTS & SYMBOLS

If you're a visual person, learning to knit lace from a chart will liberate your knitting skills. A chart is similar to a photo negative of your pattern and allows you to see how each stitch is placed in your knitting. You'll be able to see which direction a decrease leans, where a yarn over is placed, and what stitches from the previous row will be used to complete the next stitch. They'll help you keep track of where you are in a lace pattern. Regardless of your knitting skill level, eventually you'll encounter a pattern that uses charts.

LEGEND OR KEY

We have made every effort to be consistent in the symbols that we have used with the charts in this book, but stitch symbols are not universal. Each book that uses charts will have their own legend or key for the symbols in their charts. What may be the symbol for a knit stitch in this book may be something entirely different in another book.

Always carefully read through the legend or key for your chart before you begin. Keep the key nearby to refer to as often as you need. Once you become familiar with those symbols, you'll become a chart-reading pro.

READING A CHART WHILE WORKING IN THE ROUND

If your knitted piece is worked in the round, you'll always read the chart from **right** to **left** on every round. The round numbers will be on the right-hand side of the chart (see chart below). This indicates that you'll be working every round from the first stitch on the right side to the last stitch on the left side of the chart. Then, you'll begin the next round back at the right side of the chart, one square up from the last round, and repeat the process. The stitches are indicated by the numbers at the bottom of the chart.

CHART

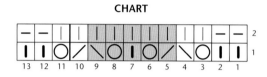

Helpful Hints: Enlarge your chart on a photocopier and use a highlighter to mark the wrong side rows. Purchase a magnetic row finder or chart keeper to hold your chart in place and keep track of the row you are working on.

READING A CHART WHILE KNITTING ROWS

When knitting flat rows, you turn your work at the end of each row. Your chart will reflect that by having the row numbers on the chart alternate from left to right. You'll always begin a row on the same side that the row number is located. The **right** side rows will be numbered on the right side and the **wrong** side rows will be numbered on the left side. This means that on the **wrong** side rows, you will be reading and working the chart from **left** to **right**.

See the Horseshoe Pattern Chart in the next column.

WORKING A REPEAT

An aspect of chart knitting that knitters can find confusing is the shaded areas on charts that are labeled "Repeat." It indicates that the shaded area is to be repeated until the number of stitches at the end of chart remain. This is just an easy way to condense a large pattern into a more manageable size.

The written instructions can differ from a chart's pattern repeat. This is usually due to the pattern having the same kind of stitch at the beginning and end of a charted repeat. For example, in the Horseshoe Stitch pattern shown below, Row 5 would be written out as "K4, YO, K1, slip 1, K2 tog, PSSO, K1, YO, ★ K5, YO, K1, K2 tog, PSSO, K1, YO; repeat from ★ across to last 4 sts, K4." The actual chart stitches with the shaded repeat inside of the braces { }, are **K1** (edge stitch), {**K3**, YO, K1, slip 1, K2 tog, PSSO, K1, YO, **K2**}, repeat the shaded area across to last 2 sts, **K2** (edge stitches).

Helpful Hints: Place a marker each time you begin a new pattern repeat to keep track of the correct number of stitches in each repeat and help you be able to spot mistakes quickly. Make sure that the marker is different in some way, in either color or shape, than the ones previously used in the pattern. You can tie a contrasting color of yarn at the end of each row repeat to help keep track of your rows, too.

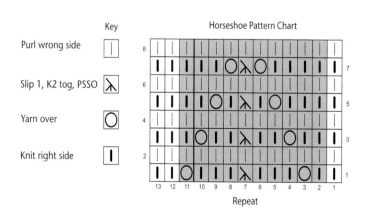

Reference Guide continued on page 6.

WHAT IF I HAVE MADE A MISTAKE?

It all depends on *where* your mistake is and *what* kind of mistake it is as to how you need to deal with it.

A common mistake made in lace knitting is a forgotten yarn over. If that happened on the previous row, and you realized it when you got to the spot with no yarn over, you can simply pick up the strand of yarn between the stitches (*Fig. A*) to be your yarn over and work it by either knitting or purling it as you would have worked the yarn over.

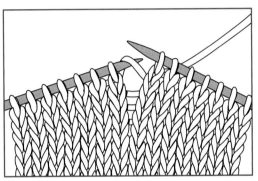

Fig. A

But, if you found that same mistake several rows or rounds below, that's a whole lot harder to correct. You can work backwards, removing the stitches one by one or you can rip out the rows. Ripping out lace is very hard to do with all the yarn overs, but it can be done.

LIFELINES

To make your knitting lace experience a little more secure and less frustrating, use a "lifeline" as you knit. A lifeline can be a strand of yarn like the red yarn in Photo A below, a smaller size circular needle, also in Photo A, or a smaller size double pointed needle. Pull your lifeline through the stitches of any row after you have completed it.

Put point protectors on the needle points so they won't slip out. Keep checking your knitting and moving your lifeline up as you go, so if you do find a mistake, you can rip back to the lifeline, only losing a few rows. It's also a good idea to make a note of what row you have your lifeline on. You may eventually have the pattern memorized, but a little written back-up never hurts!

Photo A

BLOCKING LACE

Not all the pieces in this leaflet need to be blocked, but most have an unblocked and a blocked measurement. Blocking isn't a difficult process, but it is necessary to bring out the magic in a finished lace piece. Some of the designs take more blocking than others to get the desired measurements. When blocking a piece, take into consideration the fiber content of the yarn. Is the yarn made from natural fibers, such as cotton, wool, silk? Or man-made fibers, acrylic, rayon? Natural fibers and even blends of natural and man-made fibers tend to block more easily.

There are two basic methods of blocking; pin blocking and wire blocking. For either you'll need a flat, padded surface that is clean and colorfast. This can be a carpeted area, a cardboard cutting board with an inch grid marked on it, the dense foam puzzle pieces that are used to cushion children's play areas, or even a mattress with an old sheet on it for larger projects. A yardstick, a ruler and straight pins or rust proof T-pins are essential tools for blocking with both of these techniques.

Your project needs to be damp (not thoroughly wet). You can remove the excess water by putting it through a few minutes on the spin cycle of your washer, or you can put it in a towel and press out the excess water. Either way is fine, but the towel method is preferable on larger projects to prevent them from drying faster than you can block.

Gather your supplies and let's get started.

PIN BLOCKING

The simplest blocking method is pin blocking. The Bookmark on page 9 has the steps for pin blocking.

> *Helpful Hint:* If your lace piece has a scalloped edging, count the number of points and divide the total by 4. Make sure each section has the same number of points between each mark on your blocking surface.

Place a pin every inch or so on a straight edge, more often on a curved edge. Place a pin in each point of a scalloped or pointed edging. Stand back and check the shape periodically, correcting where needed. Use a ruler to make sure that points or scalloped edges are stretched apart equally.

Let dry completely.

WIRE BLOCKING

Wire blocking uses the same tools as pin blocking plus a set of blocking wires. Using wires makes blocking easier and quicker. A wire is slipped through the edges of your lace piece, then pins are placed along the inside of the blocking wires to hold the edges in place. When working with a scalloped or pointed edging, slip the wire through each point and pin in place.

Blocking wires can be found in your local yarn store or ordered online. If you fall in love with lace knitting, a set of blocking wires would be a good investment.

Step 1: Use a yardstick to find the center of your blocking surface. Working out from the center, divide the surface into fourths and then into eighths, marking the recommended blocked measurements at each of these points.

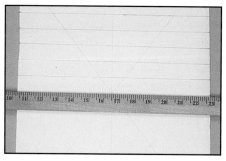

Step 1

Reference Guide continued on page 8.

Helpful Hint: If your lace piece has a scalloped edging, count the number of points and divide the total by the number of wires in your blocking set. Make sure that each wire has the same number of points.

Step 2: Dampen your project. (If you get it too wet, press it with a towel until most of the moisture is gone.) Lay the center of your project onto the center of the blocking surface and pin in place.

Step 3: Thread equal increments of the edges onto blocking wires and gently stretch out the edges, pulling as far as possible without distorting your knitting. Place pins along the inside of the blocking wires to hold in place. Gently stretch each section on wires and reposition pins until recommended blocked measurements are achieved.

Stand back and check the shape periodically, correcting where needed. Spread out points or scalloped edges equally along each wire.

Let dry completely.

Step 2

Step 3

GETTING *started*

Let's begin with a simple bookmark made with light weight yarn (2) and size 6 (1 mm) needles. You will also need a ruler, blocking pins, a small blocking board, and 20" (51 cm) length of ¹/₄" (7 mm) wide ribbon.

As with every project in this leaflet, a symbol chart of the pattern is included along with the written instructions. If you would like to try to work this pattern from the chart, start by casting on 9 sts and knitting a foundation row. Use the key to identify the stitches and follow the chart from right to left on the right side rows and from left to right on the wrong side rows. Row numbers are placed on the opposite sides of the chart—wrong side rows on the left edge and right side rows on the right edge.

When you first come to the yarn overs and the decreases, check that row in the written instructions to see the Figs. showing how to make those stitches.

Finished Size: 1⁵/₈" wide x 6" long
(4 cm x 15 cm)

Cast on 9 sts.

Foundation Row: Knit across.

Getting Started continued on page 10.

KEY

Purl wrong side	|	◯ Yarn over	
Knit wrong side	—	╱ K2 tog	
Slip 1, K2 tog, PSSO	⅄	| Knit right side	
SSK	╲		

BOOKMARK CHART

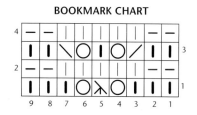

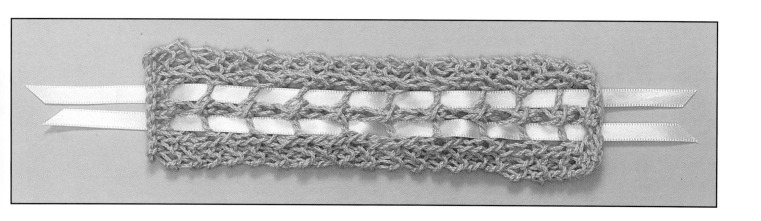

Row 1: K3,

Step 1: Yarn over,

Step 2: Slip the next stitch as if to **knit**,

Step 3: Knit the next 2 stitches together,

Step 4: Pass the slipped stitch over (Steps 2-4 are also known as *slip 1, K2 tog, PSSO*), then YO, K3 to complete the row (*Photo A*).

You have decreased two stitches, but you also made stitches with the yarn overs, so you will still have 9 stitches.

Row 2: K2, P5, K2.

Row 3: K2, K2 tog, YO, K1, YO, then

Step 5: Separately slip the next 2 stitches as if to **knit**,

Step 6: Insert the **left** needle into the **front** of both of the slipped stitches,

Step 7: Knit the two stitches together (Steps 5-7 are also known as *SSK*), then K2 to finish the row (*Photo B*).

Once again, because each yarn over is paired with a decrease, you will still have 9 stitches.

Step 1

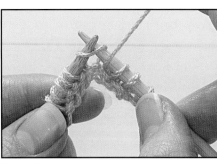

Step 2

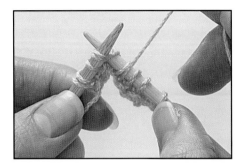

Step 3

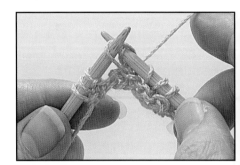

Step 4

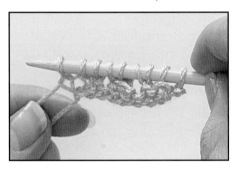

Photo A

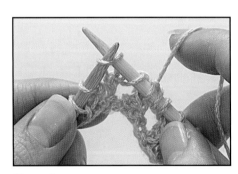

Step 5

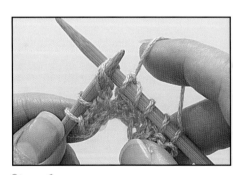

Step 6

Step 7

Photo B

Row 4: K2, P5, K2.

Repeat Rows 1-4 for pattern or follow the chart until Bookmark measures approximately 6" (15 cm), ending by working Row 1 or 3.

Last Row: Knit across.

Bind off all sts in **knit**.

FINISHING

Let's block your Bookmark using pin blocking.

Step 1: Use a ruler to find the center of your blocking surface. Working out from the center, divide the surface into fourths and then into eighths, marking the recommended blocked measurements at each of these points.

Step 2: Dampen your Bookmark. (If you get it too wet, press it with a towel until most of the moisture is gone.)

Step 3: Lay the center of your project onto the center of the blocking surface and pin in place. Place a pin every inch or so on the straight edges. Gently stretch out the edges, pulling as far as possible without distorting your knitting.

Helpful Hint: When blocking to a specified blocked measurement, start at a smaller measurement and ease out to the finished measurement to prevent distortion of stitches.

Let dry completely.

Weave an 10" (25.5 cm) length of ribbon through each vertical set of yarn overs down the center of the Bookmark. Trim ribbon ends, leaving an inch (2.5 cm) of ribbon at each end.

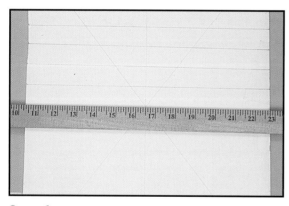

Step 1

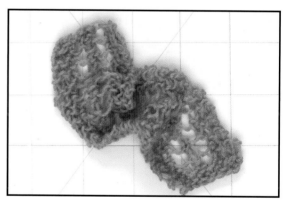

Step 2

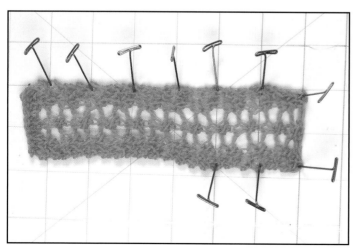

Step 3

Aren't you surprised how easy that was? Now you can knit any of these lacy projects and get great results!

QUICK *scarf*

Finished Size:
  7"w x 81"h (18 cm x 205.5 cm)

MATERIALS
  Bulky Weight Yarn 🧶**5**
    [3 ounces, 135 yards
    (85 grams, 123 meters) per ball]:
    2 balls
  Straight knitting needles, size 11
    (8 mm) **or** size needed for gauge

GAUGE: In Stockinette Stitch,
        8 sts and 10 rows = 3" (7.5 cm)

When instructed to slip a stitch,
always slip it as if to **knit**.

BODY
Cast on 21 sts.

Foundation Row: Knit across.

Begin following Chart below, if desired.

Row 1 (Right side): Slip 1, K1, K2 tog (*Fig. 3, page 73*), YO (*Fig. 11a, page 75*), K2, YO, SSK (*Figs. 5a-c, page 74*), K2 tog, YO, K1, YO, SSK, K2 tog, YO, K2, K2 tog, YO, K2.

Row 2 AND ALL WRONG SIDE ROWS: Slip 1, K1, K2 tog, YO, P 13, K2 tog, YO, K2.

Row 3: Slip 1, K1, K2 tog, YO, K2, YO, SSK, K2 tog, YO, K1, YO, SSK, K2 tog, YO, K2, K2 tog, YO, K2.

KEY

Purl wrong side	⊡
Knit wrong side	⊟
Slip 1, K2 tog, PSSO	⋏
SSK	⧄
Yarn over	◯
K2 tog	⧸
Knit right side	I
Slip 1	S

CHART

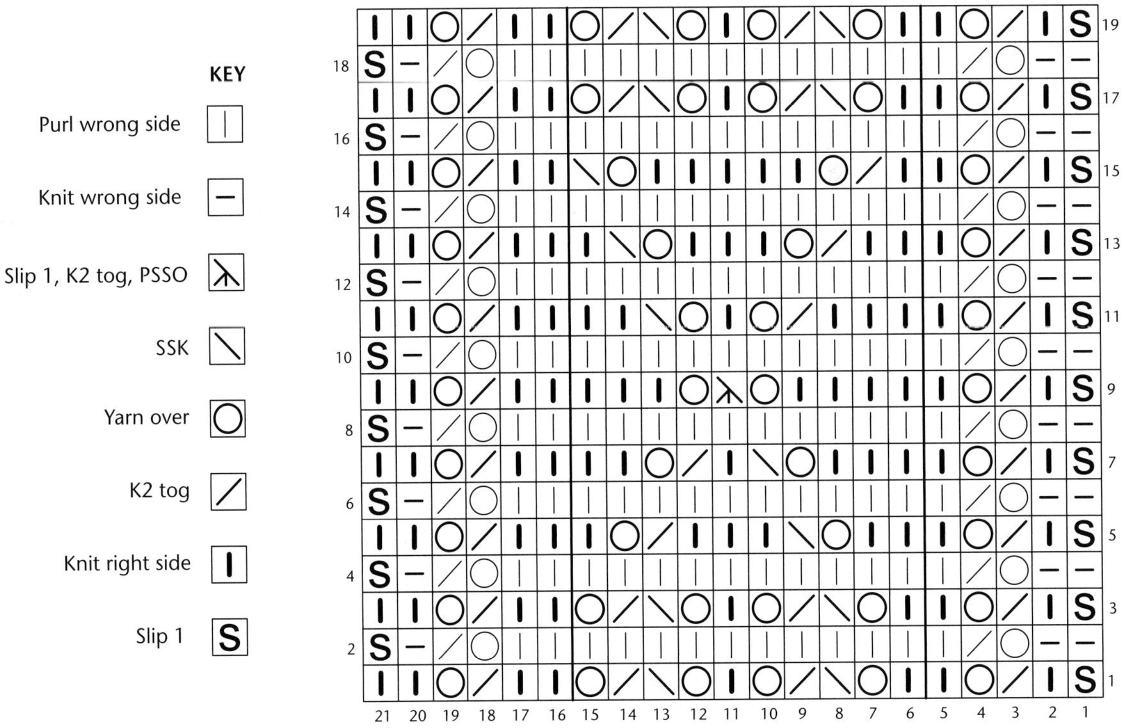

Repeat Rows 4-19 of Chart for pattern.

Row 5: Slip 1, K1, K2 tog, YO, K3, YO, SSK, K3, K2 tog, YO, K3, K2 tog, YO, K2.

Row 7: Slip 1, K1, K2 tog, YO, K4, YO, SSK, K1, K2 tog, YO, K4, K2 tog, YO, K2.

Row 9: Slip 1, K1, K2 tog, YO, K5, YO, [slip 1, K2 tog, PSSO *(Figs. 6a & b, page 74)*], YO, K5, K2 tog, YO, K2.

Row 11: Slip 1, K1, K2 tog, YO, K4, K2 tog, YO, K1, YO, SSK, K4, K2 tog, YO, K2.

Row 13: Slip 1, K1, K2 tog, YO, K3, K2 tog, YO, K3, YO, SSK, K3, K2 tog, YO, K2.

Row 15: Slip 1, K1, K2 tog, YO, K2, K2 tog, YO, K5, YO, SSK, K2, K2 tog, YO, K2.

Row 17: Slip 1, K1, K2 tog, YO, K2, YO, SSK, K2 tog, YO, K1, YO, SSK, K2 tog, YO, K2, K2 tog, YO, K2.

Row 19: Slip 1, K1, K2 tog, YO, K2, YO, SSK, K2 tog, YO, K1, YO, SSK, K2 tog, YO, K2, K2 tog, YO, K2.

Repeat Rows 4-19 for pattern until Scarf measures approximately 80" (203 cm) from cast on edge, ending by working Row 19.

Last Row: Knit across.

Bind off all sts in **knit**.

CHEVRON STITCH *pillow*

Finished Size:
  Unblocked - 15" (38 cm) square
  Blocked - 16" (40.5 cm) square

MATERIALS 🔵 **MEDIUM 4**
  Medium Weight Yarn
    [3.5 ounces, 170 yards
    (100 grams, 156 meters)
    per ball]: 2 balls
  Straight knitting needles,
    size 10 (6 mm) **or** size
    needed for gauge
  Yarn needle
  16" (40.5 cm) Square pillow

GAUGE: In Stockinette Stitch,
      15 sts and 20 rows = 4"
      (10 cm)

FRONT
Cast on 57 sts.

Begin following Chevron Stitch
Pillow Chart, page 16, if desired.

Rows 1-3: Knit across.

Row 4 (Right side): K3, YO
(Fig. 11a, page 75), ★ SSK
(Figs. 5a-c, page 74), K8, YO;
repeat from ★ across to last 14 sts,
SSK, K7, K2 tog *(Fig. 3, page 73)*,
YO, K3.

Note: Loop a short piece of yarn around any stitch to mark Row 4 as **right** side.

Row 5 AND ALL WRONG SIDE ROWS: K2, purl across to last 2 sts, K2.

Row 6: K4, YO, SSK, K5, K2 tog, YO, ★ K1, YO, SSK, K5, K2 tog, YO; repeat from ★ across to last 4 sts, K4.

Row 8: K5, YO, SSK, K3, K2 tog, YO, ★ K3, YO, SSK, K3, K2 tog, YO; repeat from ★ across to last 5 sts, K5.

Row 10: K3, (YO, SSK, K1) twice, K2 tog, YO, ★ K2, (YO, SSK, K1) twice, K2 tog, YO; repeat from ★ across to last 6 sts, K1, K2 tog, YO, K3.

Row 12: K4, YO, SSK, K1, YO, [slip 1, K2 tog, PSSO *(Figs. 6a & b, page 74)*], YO, K1, K2 tog, YO, ★ K1, YO, SSK, K1, YO, slip 1, K2 tog, PSSO, YO, K1, K2 tog, YO; repeat from ★ across to last 4 sts, K4.

Rows 14-27: Repeat Rows 8-13 twice; then repeat Rows 8 and 9 once **more**.

Row 28: K6, YO, SSK, K1, K2 tog, YO, ★ K5, YO, SSK, K1, K2 tog, YO; repeat from ★ across to last 6 sts, K6.

Row 30: K7, ★ YO, slip 1, K2 tog, PSSO, YO, K7; repeat from ★ across.

Row 32: K3, P1, ★ SSK, K2, YO, K1, YO, K2, K2 tog, P1; repeat from ★ across to last 3 sts, K3.

Rows 34-51: Repeat Rows 32 and 33, 9 times.

Rows 52-76: Repeat Rows 6-30.

Rows 77-79: Knit across.

Bind off all sts in **knit**, leaving a long end for sewing.

CHEVRON STITCH

PINECONE STITCH

BACK

Work same as Front **or** cast on 60 sts.

Rows 1-4: Knit across.

Row 5: K2, purl across to last 2 sts, K2.

Row 6: Knit across.

Repeat Rows 5 and 6 for pattern until Back measures 15³/₄" (40 cm) from cast on edge, ending by working Row 5.

Last 4 Rows: Knit across.

Bind off all sts in **knit**.

FINISHING

Block pieces to desired measurements.

With **wrong** sides of Front and Back together, sew pieces together, inserting pillow before closing.

CHEVRON STITCH PILLOW CHART

KEY

|	Purl wrong side
—	Knit wrong side
人	Slip 1, K2 tog, PSSO
\	SSK
O	Yarn over
/	K2 tog
I	Knit right side
▬	Purl right side

Work the first edge stitches, then repeat the stitches in the shaded area for pattern (Rows 4-51), ending with working the remaining edge stitches.

Repeat Rows 6-30 of Chart for pattern.

16 CHEVRON *pillow*

PINECONE STITCH *Pillow*

Shown on page 15.

■■□□ **EASY**

Finished Size:
Unblocked - 15" (38 cm) square
Blocked - 16" (40.5 cm) square

MATERIALS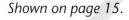
Medium Weight Yarn
[3.5 ounces, 170 yards
(100 grams, 156 meters)
per ball]: 2 balls
Straight knitting needles, size 10
(6 mm) **or** size needed for
gauge
Yarn needle
16" (40.5 cm) Square pillow

GAUGE: In Stockinette Stitch,
15 sts and 20 rows = 4"
(10 cm)

FRONT
Cast on 57 sts.

Begin following Pinecone Stitch
Pillow Chart, page 18, if desired.

Rows 1-3: Knit across.

Row 4 (Right side)**:** K4, SSK
(Figs. 5a-c, page 74), K2, YO
(Fig. 11a, page 75), K1, YO, K2,
K2 tog *(Fig. 3, page 73)*, ★ K1,
SSK, K2, YO, K1, YO, K2, K2 tog;
repeat from ★ across to last 4 sts,
K4.

Note: Loop a short piece of yarn around any stitch to mark Row 4 as **right** side.

Row 5 AND ALL WRONG SIDE ROWS: K2, purl across to last 2 sts, K2.

Rows 6-9: Repeat Rows 4 and 5 twice.

Row 10: K4, YO, SSK, K5, K2 tog, YO, ★ K1, YO, SSK, K5, K2 tog, YO; repeat from ★ across to last 4 sts, K4.

Row 12: K5, YO, SSK, K3, K2 tog, YO, ★ K3, YO, SSK, K3, K2 tog, YO; repeat from ★ across to last 5 sts, K5.

Row 14: K6, YO, SSK, K1, K2 tog, YO, ★ K5, YO, SSK, K1, K2 tog, YO; repeat from ★ across to last 6 sts, K6.

Row 16: K4, YO, K2, K2 tog, K1, SSK, K2, YO, ★ K1, YO, K2, K2 tog, K1, SSK, K2, YO; repeat from ★ across to last 4 sts, K4.

Rows 18-21: Repeat Rows 16 and 17 twice.

Row 22: K6, K2 tog, YO, K1, YO, SSK, ★ K5, K2 tog, YO, K1, YO, SSK; repeat from ★ across to last 6 sts, K6.

Row 24: K5, K2 tog, YO, K3, YO, SSK, ★ K3, K2 tog, YO, K3, YO, SSK; repeat from ★ across to last 5 sts, K5.

Row 26: K4, K2 tog, YO, K5, YO, SSK, ★ K1, K2 tog, YO, K5, YO, SSK; repeat from ★ across to last 4 sts, K4.

Rows 28-74: Repeat Rows 4-27 once, then repeat Rows 4-26 once **more**.

Rows 75-77: Knit across.

Bind off all sts in **knit**, leaving a long end for sewing.

Instructions continued on page 18.

PINECONE STITCH *Pillow*   **17**

BACK

Work same as Front **or** cast on 60 sts.

Rows 1-4: Knit across.

Row 5: K2, purl across to last 2 sts, K2.

Row 6: Knit across.

Repeat Rows 5 and 6 for pattern until Back measures 15³/₄" (40 cm) from cast on edge, ending by working Row 5.

Last 4 Rows: Knit across.

Bind off all sts in **knit**.

FINISHING

Block pieces to desired measurements.

With **wrong** sides of Front and Back together, sew pieces together inserting pillow before closing.

KEY

⊡	Purl wrong side
—	Knit wrong side
\	SSK
◯	Yarn over
/	K2 tog
I	Knit right side

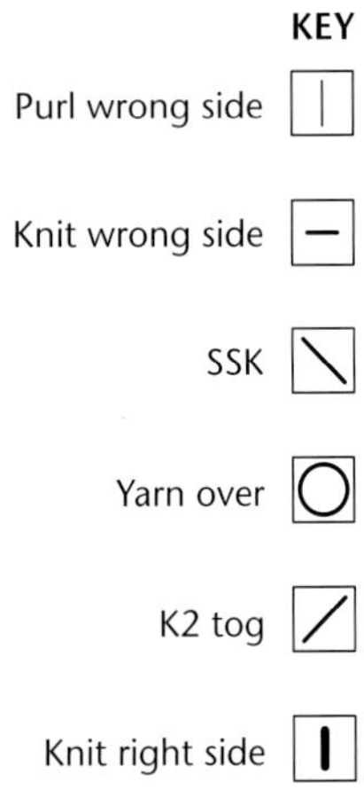

Work the first edge stitches, then repeat the stitches in the shaded area for pattern (Rows 4-27), ending with working the remaining edge stitches.

Repeat Rows 4-27 of Chart for pattern.

PINECONE STITCH PILLOW CHART

Chart rows numbered 1–27 (odd on left, even on right); columns numbered 17 down to 1 along the bottom.

EYELET *shrug*

Instructions begin on page 20.

EYELET *Shrug*

■■□□ **EASY**

Finished Size	Chest Measurement
X-Small	28-30"/(71-76 cm)
Small	32-34"/(81.5-86.5 cm)
Medium	36-38"/(91.5-96.5 cm)
Large	40-42"/(101.5-106.5 cm)
X-Large	44-46"/(112-117 cm)

Size Note: Instructions are written with sizes X-Small and Small in first set of braces { } and with sizes Medium, Large, and X-Large in second set of braces. Instructions will be easier to read if you circle all the numbers pertaining to your size. If only one number is given, it applies to all sizes.

MATERIALS
Fine Weight Yarn
  [4 ounces, 335 yards
  (113 grams, 306 meters) per skein]:
    Aqua - {1-2}{2-2-2} skeins
    (shown on page 21)
          OR
  [6 ounces, 410 yards
  (150 grams, 375 meters) per skein]:
    Blue - {1-1}{2-2-2} skeins
    (shown on page 19)
Straight knitting needles, size 7 (4.5 mm)
  or size needed for gauge
Yarn needle

GAUGE: In Stockinette Stitch,
    20 sts and 26 rows = 4" (10 cm)

FIRST HALF
Cast on {67-67}{77-77-87} sts **loosely**.

Begin following Chart A, if desired.

Row 1: Purl across.

Row 2 (Right side)**:** K6, K2 tog (*Fig. 3, page 73*), YO (*Fig. 11a, page 75*), K1, YO, SSK (*Figs. 5a-c, page 74*), ★ K5, K2 tog, YO, K1, YO, SSK; repeat from ★ across to last 6 sts, K6.

Note: Loop a short piece of yarn around any stitch to mark Row 2 as **right** side.

Rows 3 thru {67-67}{79-79-91}: Repeat Rows 1 and 2, {32-32}{38-38-44} times; then repeat Row 1 once **more**.

Decrease Row: SSK, K4, K2 tog, YO, K1, YO, SSK, ★ K5, K2 tog, YO, K1, YO, SSK; repeat from ★ across to last 6 sts, K4, K2 tog: {65-65}{75-75-85} sts.

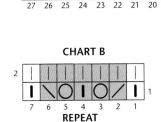

Work the first edge stitch(es), then repeat the stitches in the shaded area for pattern, ending with working the remaining edge stitch(es).

Maintaining pattern, continue to decrease one stitch at **each** edge, in same manner every 12 rows, 4 times: {57-57}{67-67-77} sts.

Work even until First Half measures {21¹/₂-22¹/₂}{23-23¹/₂-25}"/{54.5-57}{58.5-59.5-63.5} cm from cast on edge **or** 3" (7.5 cm) less than desired length of sleeve, ending by working a **purl** row.

EDGING

Begin following Chart B, page 20, if desired.

Row 1: K1, (K2 tog, YO, K1, YO, SSK) across to last st, K1.

Row 2: Purl across.

Repeat Rows 1 and 2 until Edging measures 3" (7.5 cm), ending by working Row 2.

Last Row: K1, K2 tog, YO, K1, YO, SSK, ★ YO, K2 tog, YO, K1, YO, SSK; repeat from ★ across to last st, K1: {67-67}{79-79-91} sts.

Bind off all sts as follows: K2, return the 2 sts just knit back on to left needle, K2 tog tbl (*Fig. 4, page 74*), ★ K1, return the 2 sts on right needle back on to left needle, K2 tog tbl; repeat from ★ across; finish off leaving a long end for sewing.

SECOND HALF
Work same as First Half.

FINISHING
With **right** sides of both pieces together, sew cast on edges together.

With **right** sides together, sew each sleeve seam {16¹/₂-16¹/₂}{17-17-17¹/₂}"/{42-42}{43-43-44.5} cm from bound off edge of Edging.

Note: The Table Runner is worked in panels of pattern stitches with a top and a bottom edging.

◼◼◼◻ **INTERMEDIATE**

Finished Size:
Unblocked - 12^1/$_4$"w x 35^1/$_2$"h (31 cm x 90 cm)
Blocked - 14^1/$_2$"w x 43"h (37 cm x 109 cm)

MATERIALS
Fine Weight Yarn ![FINE 2]
[1.75 ounces, 136 yards
(50 grams, 125 meters) per ball]: 3 balls
Straight knitting needles, size 7 (4.5 mm) **or**
size needed for gauge
Markers

GAUGE: In Stockinette Stitch,
20 sts and 26 rows = 4" (10 cm)

Remember that the Table Runner will
stretch approximately 20% when blocked.

When instructed to slip a stitch, always slip
it as if to **knit**.

TOP CHEVRON EYELET EDGING

Cast on 17 sts.

Foundation Row: K6, P9, K2.

Begin following Top Chevron Edging Chart,
page 24, if desired.

Row 1 (Right side)**:** K2, YO, [K2 tog (*Fig. 3,
page 73*), YO (*Fig. 11a, page 75*)] 3 times, K2,
(K2 tog, YO) twice, K3: 18 sts.

Note: Loop a short piece of yarn around
any stitch to mark Row 1 as **right** side.

Row 2: Slip 1, K2 tog, YO, K3, P 10, K2.

Row 3: K2, YO, (K2 tog, YO) 3 times, K3,
(K2 tog, YO) twice, K3: 19 sts.

Row 4: Slip 1, K2 tog, YO, K3, P 11, K2.

Row 5: K2, YO, (K2 tog, YO) 3 times, K4,
(K2 tog, YO) twice, K3: 20 sts.

Row 6: Slip 1, K2 tog, YO, K3, P 12, K2.

Row 7: K2, YO, (K2 tog, YO) 3 times, K5,
(K2 tog, YO) twice, K3: 21 sts.

Row 8: Slip 1, K2 tog, YO, K3, P 13, K2.

Instructions continued on page 24.

Row 9: K1, SSK (*Figs. 5a-c, page 74*), (YO, SSK) 4 times, K3, (K2 tog, YO) twice, K3: 20 sts.

Row 10: Slip 1, K2 tog, YO, K3, P 12, K2.

Row 11: K1, SSK, (YO, SSK) 4 times, K2, (K2 tog, YO) twice, K3: 19 sts.

Row 12: Slip 1, K2 tog, YO, K3, P 11, K2.

Row 13: K1, SSK, (YO, SSK) 4 times, K1, (K2 tog, YO) twice, K3: 18 sts.

Row 14: Slip 1, K2 tog, YO, K3, P 10, K2.

Row 15: K1, SSK, (YO, SSK) 4 times, (K2 tog, YO) twice, K3: 17 sts.

Row 16: Slip 1, K2 tog, YO, K3, P9, K2.

Rows 17-96: Repeat Rows 1-16, 5 times.

Bind off all sts in **knit**; leaving last st on needle.

BODY

Foundation Row: With **right** side of Edging facing, pick up 60 sts evenly spaced across end of rows (*Fig. 12, page 75*): 61 sts.

Row 1: K4, P2, place marker (*see Markers, page 73*), purl across to last 5 sts, place marker, P1, K4.

Row 2: Slip 1, K1, K2 tog, YO, knit across to last marker, K2, K2 tog, YO, K2.

Row 3: Slip 1, K1, K2 tog, YO (*Fig. 11b, page 75*), purl across to last marker, P1, K2 tog, YO, K2.

Row 4: Slip 1, K1, K2 tog, YO, knit across to last marker, K2, K2 tog, YO, K2.

Row 5: Slip 1, K1, K2 tog, YO, purl across to last marker, P1, K2 tog, YO, K2.

TOP CHEVRON EDGING CHART

KEY

■	No stitch in area
□	Purl wrong side
—	Knit wrong side
\	SSK
O	Yarn over
/	K2 tog
I	Knit right side

LADDER STITCH PANEL

Begin following Ladder Stitch Panel Chart, if desired.

Row 1: Slip 1, K1, K2 tog, YO, K2, YO, SSK, K2 tog, YO, (K2, YO, SSK, K2 tog, YO) across to last marker, K2, K2 tog, YO, K2.

Row 2: Slip 1, K1, K2 tog, YO, purl across to last marker, P1, K2 tog, YO, K2.

Rows 3-14: Repeat Rows 1 and 2, 6 times.

Row 15: Slip 1, K1, K2 tog, YO, knit across to last marker, K2, K2 tog, YO, K2.

Row 16: Slip 1, K1, K2 tog, YO, purl across to last marker, P1, K2 tog, YO, K2.

Rows 17 and 18: Repeat Rows 15 and 16.

Instructions continued on page 26.

LADDER STITCH PANEL CHART

KEY

│	Purl wrong side
–	Knit wrong side
╲	SSK
○	Yarn over
╱	K2 tog
I	Knit right side
S	Slip 1

Work the first edge stitches, then repeat the stitches in the shaded area for pattern, ending with working the remaining edge stitches.

HORSESHOE STITCH PANEL

Begin following Horseshoe Stitch Panel Chart, if desired.

Row 1: Slip 1, K1, K2 tog, YO, K2, YO, K3, [slip 1, K2 tog, PSSO *(Figs. 6a & b, page 74)*], K3, YO, ★ K1, YO, K3, slip 1, K2 tog, PSSO, K3, YO; repeat from ★ across to last marker, K2, K2 tog, YO, K2.

Row 2: Slip 1, K1, K2 tog, YO, purl across to last marker, P1, K2 tog, YO, K2.

Row 3: Slip 1, K1, K2 tog, YO, K3, ★ YO, K2, slip 1, K2 tog, PSSO, K2, YO, K3; repeat from ★ across to last 4 sts, K2 tog, YO, K2.

Row 4: Slip 1, K1, K2 tog, YO, purl across to last marker, P1, K2 tog, YO, K2.

Row 5: Slip 1, K1, K2 tog, YO, K4, YO, K1, slip 1, K2 tog, PSSO, K1, YO, ★ K5, YO, K1, slip 1, K2 tog, PSSO, K1, YO; repeat from ★ across last 8 sts, K4, K2 tog, YO, K2.

Row 6: Slip 1, K1, K2 tog, YO, purl across to last marker, P1, K2 tog, YO, K2.

Row 7: Slip 1, K1, K2 tog, YO, K5, YO, slip 1, K2 tog, PSSO, YO, ★ K7, YO, slip 1, K2 tog, PSSO, YO; repeat from ★ across to last 9 sts, K5, K2 tog, YO, K2.

Row 8: Slip 1, K1, K2 tog, YO, purl across to last marker, P1, K2 tog, YO, K2.

Rows 9-16: Repeat Rows 1-8.

Row 17: Slip 1, K1, K2 tog, YO, knit across to last marker, K2, K2 tog, YO, K2.

Row 18: Slip 1, K1, K2 tog, YO, purl across to last marker, P1, K2 tog, YO, K2.

Rows 19 and 20: Repeat Rows 17 and 18.

Work the first edge stitches, then repeat the stitches in the shaded area for pattern, ending with working the remaining edge stitches.

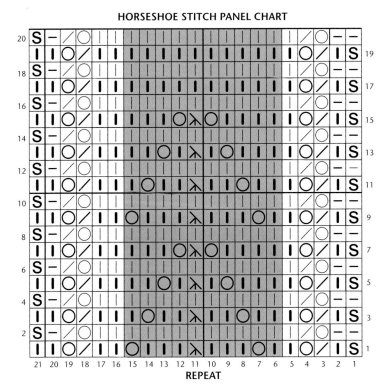

HORSESHOE STITCH PANEL CHART

KEY

Purl wrong side — [|]

Knit wrong side — [−]

Slip 1, K2 tog, PSSO — [⅄]

Yarn over — [○]

SSK — [╱]

Knit right side — [I]

REPEAT

DIAMOND LATTICE PANEL

Begin following Diamond Lattice Panel Chart, if desired.

Row 1: Slip 1, K1, K2 tog, YO, K2, YO, SSK, K2 tog, YO, (K1, YO, SSK, K2 tog, YO) across to last marker, K2, K2 tog, YO, K2.

Row 2 AND ALL WRONG SIDE ROWS: Slip 1, K1, K2 tog, YO, purl across to last marker, P1, K2 tog, YO, K2.

Rows 3 and 4: Repeat Rows 1 and 2.

Row 5: Slip 1, K1, K2 tog, YO, K3, YO, SSK, K3, K2 tog, YO, K3, (YO, SSK, K3, K2 tog, YO, K3) across last 4 sts, K2 tog, YO, K2.

Row 7: Slip 1, K1, K2 tog, YO, K4, YO, SSK, K1, K2 tog, YO, (K5, YO, SSK, K1, K2 tog, YO) across to last 8 sts, K4, K2 tog, YO, K2.

Row 9: Slip 1, K1, K2 tog, YO, K5, YO, slip 1, K2 tog, PSSO, YO, (K7, YO, slip 1, K2 tog, PSSO, YO) across to last 9 sts, K5, K2 tog, YO, K2.

Row 11: Slip 1, K1, K2 tog, YO, K4, K2 tog, YO, K1, YO, SSK, (K5, K2 tog, YO, K1, YO, SSK) across to last 8 sts, K4, K2 tog, YO, K2.

Row 13: Slip 1, K1, K2 tog, YO, K3, (K2 tog, YO, K3, YO, SSK, K3) across to last 4 sts, K2 tog, YO, K2.

Row 15: Slip 1, K1, K2 tog, YO, K2, K2 tog, YO, K5, YO, SSK, (K1, K2 tog, YO, K5, YO, SSK) across to last marker, K2, K2 tog, YO, K2.

Rows 17-20: Repeat Rows 1 and 2 twice.

Row 21: Slip 1, K1, K2 tog, YO, knit across to last marker, K2, K2 tog, YO, K2.

Rows 23 and 24: Repeat Rows 21 and 22.

Instructions continued on page 28.

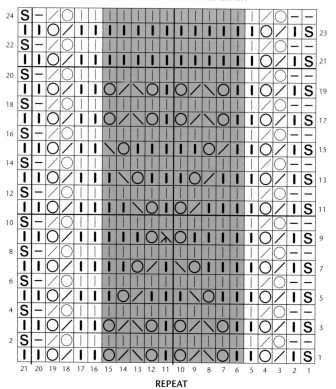

DIAMOND LATTICE PANEL CHART

REPEAT

KEY

⊓	Purl wrong side
—	Knit wrong side
⋌	Slip 1, K2 tog, PSSO
⟍	SSK
○	Yarn over
╱	K2 tog
S	Slip 1
I	Knit right side

Work the first edge stitches, then repeat the stitches in the shaded area for pattern, ending with working the remaining edge stitches.

CHEVRON PANEL

Begin following Chevron Panel Chart, page 29, if desired.

Row 1: Slip 1, K1, K2 tog, YO, K2, YO, SSK, K5, K2 tog, YO, (K1, YO, SSK, K5, K2 tog, YO) across to last 6 sts, K2, K2 tog, YO, K2.

Row 2 AND ALL WRONG SIDE ROWS: Slip 1, K1, K2 tog, YO, purl across to last marker, P1, K2 tog, YO, K2.

Row 3: Slip 1, K1, K2 tog, YO, K3, (YO, SSK, K3, K2 tog, YO, K3) across to last 4 sts, K2 tog, YO, K2.

Row 5: Slip 1, K1, K2 tog, YO, K1, (YO, SSK, K1) twice, K2 tog, YO, ★ K2, (YO, SSK, K1) twice, K2 tog, YO; repeat from ★ across to last 8 sts, (K1, K2 tog, YO) twice, K2.

Row 7: Slip 1, K1, K2 tog, YO, K2, YO, SSK, K1, YO, slip 1, K2 tog, PSSO, YO, K1, K2 tog, YO, ★ K1, YO, SSK, K1, YO, slip 1, K2 tog, PSSO, YO, K1, K2 tog, YO; repeat from ★ across to last marker, K2, K2 tog, YO, K2.

Row 9: Slip 1, K1, K2 tog, YO, K3, (YO, SSK, K3, K2 tog, YO, K3) across to last 4 sts, K2 tog, YO, K2.

Row 11: Slip 1, K1, K2 tog, YO, K4, YO, SSK, K1, K2 tog, YO, (K5, YO, SSK, K1, K2 tog, YO) across to last 8 sts, K4, K2 tog, YO, K2.

Row 13: Slip 1, K1, K2 tog, YO, K5, YO, slip 1, K2 tog, PSSO, YO, (K7, YO, slip 1, K2 tog, PSSO, YO) across to last 9 sts, K5, K2 tog, YO, K2.

Row 15: Slip 1, K1, K2 tog, YO, K1, ★ P1, SSK, K2, YO, K1, YO, K2, K2 tog; repeat from ★ across to last marker, P1, K1, K2 tog, YO, K2.

Rows 17-26: Repeat Rows 15 and 16, 5 times.

Rows 27-40: Repeat Rows 1-14.

Row 41: Slip 1, K1, K2 tog, YO, knit across to last marker, K2, K2 tog, YO, K2.

Rows 43 and 44: Repeat Rows 41 and 42.

DIAMOND LATTICE PANEL
Repeat Rows 1-24 of Diamond Lattice Panel, page 27.

HORSESHOE STITCH PANEL
Repeat Rows 1-20 of Horseshoe Stitch Panel, page 26.

LADDER STITCH PANEL
Repeat Rows 1-17 of Ladder Stitch Panel, page 25.

When working next row, remove all markers.

Last Row: K4, [P2, P2 tog (*Fig. 7, page 74*)] 13 times, P1, K4: 48 sts.

Instructions continued on page 30.

CHEVRON PANEL CHART

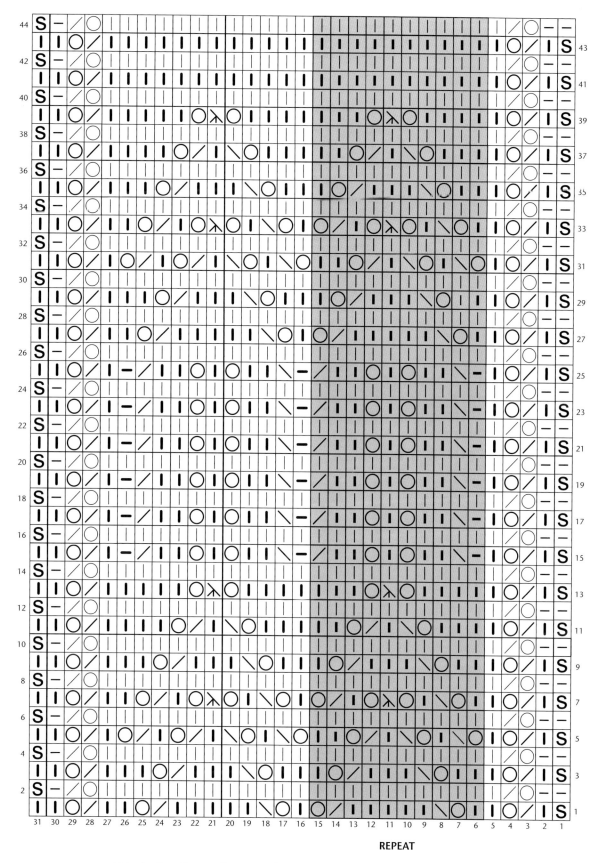

KEY

⊔	Purl wrong side
−	Knit wrong side
⋏	Slip 1, K2 tog, PSSO
╲	SSK
○	Yarn over
╱	K2 tog
S	Slip 1
I	Knit right side
▬	Purl right side

REPEAT

Work the first edge stitches, then repeat the stitches in the shaded area for pattern, ending with working the remaining edge stitches.

BOTTOM CHEVRON EDGING

Add 17 sts onto working needle (*Figs. 10a & b, page 75*).

Begin following Bottom Chevron Edging Chart, page 31, if desired.

Row 1 (Right side)**:** K2, YO, (K2 tog, YO) 3 times, K2, (K2 tog, YO) twice, K2, knit last st of Edging and next st of Body together, leave remaining sts unworked: 18 sts on right needle.

Row 2: Turn; K1, K2 tog, YO, K3, P 10, K2.

Row 3: K2, YO, (K2 tog, YO) 3 times, K3, (K2 tog, YO) twice, K2, knit last st of Edging and next st of Body together, leave remaining sts unworked: 19 sts on right needle.

Row 4: Turn; K1, K2 tog, YO, K3, P 11, K2.

Row 5: K2, YO, (K2 tog, YO) 3 times, K4, (K2 tog, YO) twice, K2, knit last st of Edging and next st of Body together, leave remaining sts unworked: 20 sts on right needle.

Row 6: Turn; K1, K2 tog, YO, K3, P 12, K2.

Row 7: K2, YO, (K2 tog, YO) 3 times, K5, (K2 tog, YO) twice, K2, knit last st of Edging and next st of Body together, leave remaining sts unworked: 21 sts on right needle.

Row 8: Turn; K1, K2 tog, YO, K3, P 13, K2.

Row 9: K1, SSK, (YO, SSK) 4 times, K3, (K2 tog, YO) twice, K2, knit last st of Edging and next st of Body together, leave remaining sts unworked: 20 sts on right needle.

Row 10: Turn; K1, K2 tog, YO, K3, P 12, K2.

Row 11: K1, SSK, (YO, SSK) 4 times, K2, (K2 tog, YO) twice, K2, knit last st of Edging and next st of Body together, leave remaining sts unworked: 19 sts on right needle.

Row 12: Turn; K1, K2 tog, YO, K3, P 11, K2.

Row 13: K1, SSK, (YO, SSK) 4 times, K1, (K2 tog, YO) twice, K2, knit last st of Edging and next st of Body together, leave remaining sts unworked: 18 sts on right needle.

Row 14: **Turn;** K1, K2 tog, YO, K3, P 10, K2.

Row 15: K1, SSK, (YO, SSK) 4 times, (K2 tog, YO) twice, K2, knit last st of Edging and next st of Body together, leave remaining sts unworked: 17 sts on right needle.

Row 16: **Turn;** K1, K2 tog, YO, K3, P9, K2.

Repeat Rows 1-16 until all sts of the Body are used, ending by working Row 16.

Bind off all sts in **knit.**

Care and Blocking Instructions: Gently hand wash Table Runner and place on spin cycle in washer to remove excess water. Pin out to blocked dimensions on a clean surface. Let dry completely.

BOTTOM CHEVRON EDGING CHART

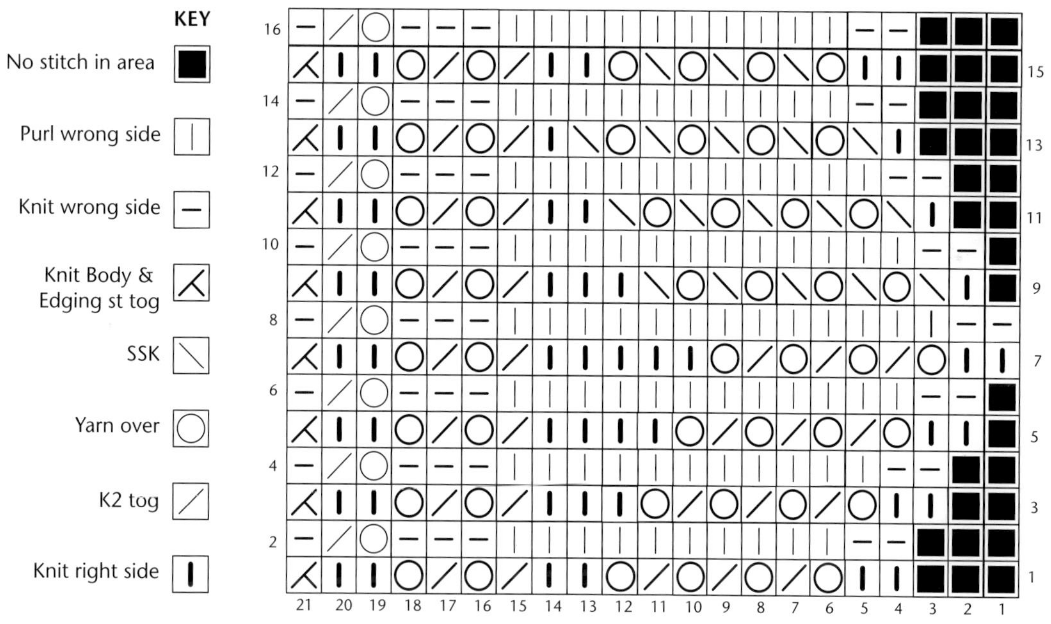

KEY

■	No stitch in area
│	Purl wrong side
—	Knit wrong side
⟋ (boxed K)	Knit Body & Edging st tog
╲	SSK
◯	Yarn over
╱	K2 tog
I	Knit right side

CHRISTENING *blanket or shawl*

■■■□ INTERMEDIATE

Finished Size:
   Unblocked - 36" (91.5 cm) diameter
   Blocked - 48" (122 cm) diameter

MATERIALS
   Light Weight Yarn **3** LIGHT
   [6 ounces, 490 yards (170 grams,
   448 meters) per skein]:
      White - 2 skeins
            OR
   [1.75 ounces, 137 yards (50 grams,
   125 meters) per ball]:
      Pink - 6 balls (shown on page 37)
   Double pointed knitting needles, size 7
   (4.5 mm) (set of 4) **or** size needed
   for gauge
   16" (40.5 cm), 24" (61 cm) **and** 30"
   (76 cm) Circular knitting needles,
   size 7 (4.5 mm)
   Point protector
   Markers

GAUGE: In Stockinette Stitch,
         18 sts and 24 rows = 4" (10 cm)

BODY
Cast 9 sts onto a double pointed needle;
divide 3 sts onto each of 2 other double
pointed needles: 3 sts on **each** needle,
9 sts total.

   Note: Place a marker at the
   first cast on stitch to mark the
   beginning of the round *(see
   Markers, page 73)*. Begin working
   in rounds, making sure that the
   first round is not twisted *(see
   Knitting in the Round, page 73)*.

Rnd 1: Knit across each needle.

When working the next round, do **not** forget to
work the YO at the end of each needle.

Rnd 2: [K1, YO *(Fig. 11a, page 75)*] across each
needle: 6 sts on **each** needle, 18 sts total.

Rnds 3-5: Knit around.

When working the next round, do **not** forget to
work the YO at the end of each needle.

Rnd 6: (K1, YO) across each needle: 12 sts on **each**
needle, 36 sts total.

Rnds 7-12: Knit around.

When working the next round, do **not** forget to
work the YO at the end of each needle.

Rnd 13: (K1, YO) across each needle: 24 sts on **each**
needle, 72 sts total.

Rnds 14-19: Knit around.

Rnd 20: [K 11, increase in next st *(Figs. 9a & b,
page 75)*, K 12] across each needle: 25 sts on **each**
needle, 75 sts total.

Rnds 21-25: Knit around.

At this point you may be able to replace the
double pointed needles with a 16" (40.5 cm)
circular needle. When working the next round,
place markers as indicated, making sure that the
beginning marker is a different color/type than
all the other markers.

Change to longer circular needles as needed.

Instructions continued on page 34.

Rnd 26: Working sts off double pointed needles onto circular needle, (K1, YO) around, placing a marker after every 30 sts: 30 sts in **each** section, 150 sts total.

Rnds 27-31: Knit around.

Begin following Chart A, if desired.

Rnd 32: K7, YO, SSK (*Figs. 5a-c, page 74*), (K 13, YO, SSK) around to last 6 sts, K6.

Rnd 33: Knit around.

Rnd 34: K5, K2 tog (*Fig. 3, page 73*), YO, K1, YO, SSK, (K 10, K2 tog, YO, K1, YO, SSK) around to last 5 sts, K5.

Rnd 35: Knit around.

Rnd 36: K4, K2 tog, YO, K3, YO, SSK, (K8, K2 tog, YO, K3, YO, SSK) around to last 4 sts, K4.

Rnd 37: Knit around.

Rnd 38: K3, K2 tog, YO, K5, YO, SSK, (K6, K2 tog, YO, K5, YO, SSK) around to last 3 sts, K3.

Rnd 39: Knit around.

Rnd 40: K2, K2 tog, YO, K7, YO, SSK, (K4, K2 tog, YO, K7, YO, SSK) around to last 2 sts, K2.

Rnd 41: Knit around.

Rnd 42: K2, YO, SSK, K7, K2 tog, YO, (K4, YO, SSK, K7, K2 tog, YO) around to last 2 sts, K2.

Rnd 43: Knit around.

Rnd 44: K3, YO, SSK, K2, YO, SSK, K1, K2 tog, YO, ★ K6, YO, SSK, K2, YO, SSK, K1, K2 tog, YO; repeat from ★ around to last 3 sts, K3.

Rnd 45: Knit around.

Rnd 46: K4, YO, [slip 1, K2 tog, PSSO (*Figs. 6a & b, page 74*)], YO, K1, YO, slip 1, K2 tog, PSSO, YO, ★ K8, YO, slip 1, K2 tog, PSSO, YO, K1, YO, slip 1, K2 tog, PSSO, YO; repeat from ★ around to last 4 sts, K4.

Rnds 47-50: Knit around.

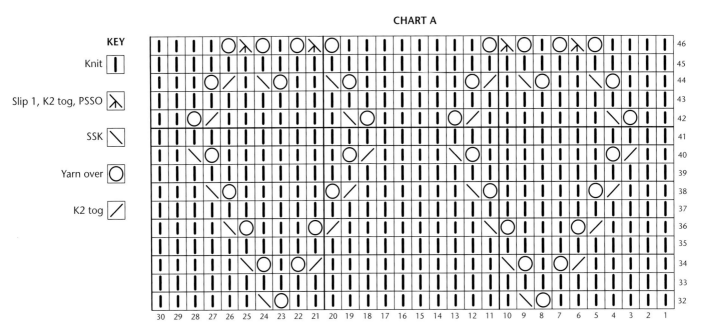

CHART A

KEY

Knit |

Slip 1, K2 tog, PSSO

SSK

Yarn over

K2 tog

Working from **right** to **left** on all rounds, work across Chart A for each section.

Rnd 51: (K1, YO) around, placing additional markers after every 30 sts: 30 sts in **each** section, 300 sts total.

Rnds 52-56: Knit around.

Begin following Chart B, if desired.

Rnd 57: (K1, YO, SSK, K2 tog, YO) around.

Rnd 58: Knit around.

Rnds 59-73: Repeat Rnds 57 and 58, 7 times; then repeat Rnd 57 once **more**.

Rnds 74-76: Knit around.

Rnd 77: (K 14, increase) around: 32 sts **each** section, 320 sts total.

Rnd 78: Knit around.

Cut working yarn; place point protector onto right tip of circular needle.

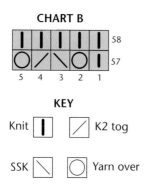

CHART B

KEY

Knit | Knit | / K2 tog |
SSK | \ | O Yarn over |

Working from **right** to **left** on all rounds, work across Chart B 6 times for each section.

EDGING

With a contrasting color of waste yarn, cast 18 sts onto left tip of circular needle.

Foundation Row: With working yarn and spare needle, K1, (K2 tog, YO) twice, SSK, (YO, SSK) twice, K2 tog, YO, K1, K2 tog, YO, K2, knit next st of Body, leave remaining sts unworked: 18 sts on right needle.

Next Row: Turn; working across Edging sts, K1, K2 tog, YO, K4, P9, K2.

Begin following Edging Chart, page 36, if desired.

When instructed to slip a stitch, always slip it as if to **knit**.

Row 1: Slip 1, K1, YO, K2 tog, YO, K1, (YO, SSK) twice, (K1, K2 tog, YO) twice, K2, knit last st of Edging and next st of Body together, leave remaining sts unworked: 19 sts on right needle.

Row 2: Turn; working across Edging sts, K1, K2 tog, YO, K4, P 10, K2.

Row 3: Slip 1, K1, YO, K2 tog, YO, K3, (YO, SSK) twice, K2 tog, YO, K1, K2 tog, YO, K2, knit last st of Edging and next st of Body together, leave remaining sts unworked: 20 sts on right needle.

Row 4: Turn; working across Edging sts, K1, K2 tog, YO, K4, P 11, K2.

Row 5: Slip 1, K1, YO, K2 tog, YO, K5, YO, SSK, (K1, K2 tog, YO) twice, K2, knit last st of Edging and next st of Body together, leave remaining sts unworked: 21 sts on right needle.

Row 6: Turn; working across Edging sts, K1, K2 tog, YO, K4, P 12, K2.

Row 7: Slip 1, K1, YO, K2 tog, YO, K7, YO, SSK, K2 tog, YO, K1, K2 tog, YO, K2, knit last st of Edging and next st of Body together, leave remaining sts unworked: 22 sts on right needle.

Instructions continued on page 36.

Row 8: Turn; working across Edging sts, K1, K2 tog, YO, K4, P 13, K2.

Row 9: Slip 1, K1, YO, SSK, YO, K9, YO, (K1, K2 tog, YO) twice, K2, knit last st of Edging and next st of Body together, leave remaining sts unworked: 24 sts on right needle.

Row 10: Turn; working across Edging sts, K1, K2 tog, YO, K4, P 15, K2.

Row 11: Slip 1, SSK, (YO, SSK) twice, K2 tog, YO, K1, YO, (SSK, K2 tog, YO) twice, K1, K2 tog, YO, K2, knit last st of Edging and next st of Body together, leave remaining sts unworked: 22 sts on right needle.

Row 12: Turn; working across Edging sts, K1, K2 tog, YO, K4, P3, P2 tog tbl *(Fig. 8, page 75)*, P3, P2 tog *(Fig. 7, page 74)*, P2, K2 tog, K1.

Row 13: Slip 1, K1, (YO, SSK) 4 times, (K1, K2 tog, YO) twice, K2, knit last st of Edging and next st of Body together, leave remaining sts unworked: 19 sts on right needle.

Row 14: Turn; working across Edging sts, K1, K2 tog, YO, K4, P 10, K2.

Row 15: Slip 1, (K2 tog, YO) twice, SSK, (YO, SSK) twice, K2 tog, YO, K1, K2 tog, YO, K2, knit last st of Edging and next st of Body together, leave remaining sts unworked: 18 sts on right needle.

Row 16: Turn; working across Edging sts, K1, K2 tog, YO, K4, P9, K2.

Repeat Rows 1-16 until all sts on the Body are used, ending by working Row 13.

Carefully matching sts, attach ends of Edging by grafting sts *(Figs. 13a-g, page 76)*. Remove contrasting color waste yarn.

Blocking Instructions: Hand wash in mild dish soap. Rinse gently. Place on spin cycle in washer to remove excess water. Lay out wet Blanket/Shawl to blocked dimension, pin in place. Let dry completely.

EDGING CHART

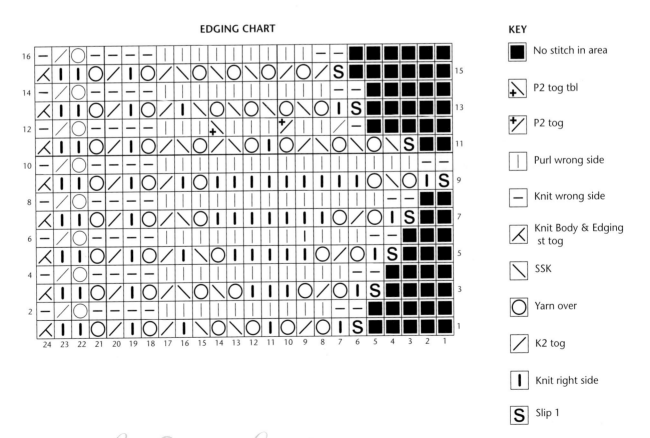

KEY

- ■ No stitch in area
- ⊬ P2 tog tbl
- ⊬ P2 tog
- | Purl wrong side
- — Knit wrong side
- ⊼ Knit Body & Edging st tog
- \ SSK
- ○ Yarn over
- / K2 tog
- | Knit right side
- S Slip 1

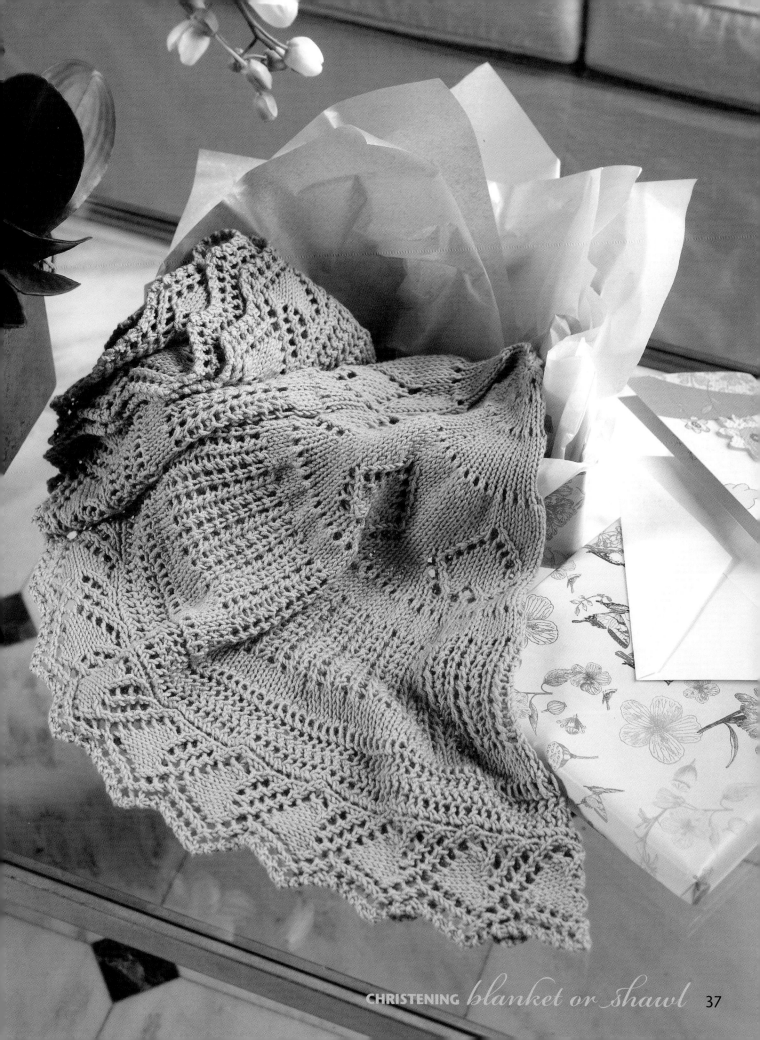

TRIANGULAR *Shawl*

Finished Size:
Unblocked - 28" x 60" (71 cm x 152.5 cm)
Blocked - 36" x 72" (91.5 cm x 183 cm)

MATERIALS
Fine Weight Yarn
[1.75 ounces, 235 yards
(50 grams, 215 meters) per ball]:
Lavender - 3 balls
OR
[.88 ounces, 227 yards
(25 grams, 208 meters) per ball]:
Black - 3 balls (shown on page 41)
Circular knitting needle, size 10 (6 mm)
or size needed for gauge
Markers

GAUGE: In Stockinette Stitch,
10 sts and 13 rows = 3" (7.5 cm)

Remember that the Shawl will stretch
25-30% when blocked.

BODY
Cast on 15 sts.

Begin following Chart A, page 40, if desired.

Row 1: Knit across.

Row 2 (Right side): K2, place marker *(see Markers, page 73)*, YO *(Fig. 11a, page 75)*, K5, YO, place marker (center st), K1, YO, K5, YO, place marker, K2: 19 sts.

Note: Loop a short piece of yarn around any stitch to mark Row 2 as **right** side.

Row 3 AND ALL WRONG SIDE ROWS: K2, purl across to within one st of center marker, purl center stitch, slip marker *(abbreviated SM)*, purl across to last marker, K2.

When working **wrong** side rows, make sure that the edge markers stay 2 stitches in from the edge and that the center marker is immediately **after** the center stitch.

Row 4: K2, SM, † YO, K1, K2 tog *(Fig. 3, page 73)*, YO, K1, YO, SSK *(Figs. 5a-c, page 74)*, K1, YO, SM †, K1, repeat from † to † once, K2: 23 sts.

Row 6: K2, SM, † YO, K2, K2 tog, YO, K1, YO, SSK, K2, YO, SM †, K1, repeat from † to † once, K2: 27 sts.

Row 8: K2, SM, † YO, K3, K2 tog, YO, K1, YO, SSK, K3, YO, SM †, K1, repeat from † to † once, K2: 31 sts.

Row 10: K2, SM, † YO, K4, K2 tog, YO, K1, YO, SSK, K4, YO, SM †, K1, repeat from † to † once, K2: 35 sts.

Row 12: K2, SM, † YO, K5, K2 tog, YO, K1, YO, SSK, K5, YO, SM †, K1, repeat from † to † once, K2: 39 sts.

Row 14: K2, SM, † YO, K6, K2 tog, YO, K1, YO, SSK, K6, YO, SM †, K1, repeat from † to † once, K2: 43 sts.

Row 16: K2, SM, † YO, K7, K2 tog, YO, K1, YO, SSK, K7, YO, SM †, K1, repeat from † to † once, K2: 47 sts.

Row 18: K2, SM, YO, K1, YO, † (SSK, K5, K2 tog, YO, K1, YO) twice, SM †, (K1, YO) twice, repeat from † to † once, K2: 51 sts.

Row 20: K2, SM, † YO, K2, YO, SSK, K5, K2 tog, YO, K1, YO, SSK, K5, K2 tog, YO, K2, YO, SM †, K1, repeat from † to † once, K2: 55 sts.

Row 22: K2, SM, † YO, K2 tog, (YO, K1, YO, SSK, K5, K2 tog) twice, YO, K1, YO, SSK, YO, SM †, K1, repeat from † to † once, K2: 59 sts.

Begin following Charts B and C, pages 42 and 43, if desired. See notes above each of these charts on how to follow them.

Row 24: K2, SM, YO, K1, K2 tog, YO, K1, YO, SSK, † K5, K2 tog, YO, K1, YO, SSK †; repeat from † to † across to within one st of center marker, K1, YO, SM, K1, YO, K1, K2 tog, YO, K1, YO, SSK, repeat from † to † across to last 3 sts, K1, YO, SM, K2: 63 sts.

Row 26: K2, SM, YO, K2, K2 tog, YO, K1, YO, SSK, † K5, K2 tog, YO, K1, YO, SSK †; repeat from † to † across to within 2 sts of center marker, K2, YO, SM, K1, YO, K2, K2 tog, YO, K1, YO, SSK, repeat from † to † across to last 4 sts, K2, YO, SM, K2: 67 sts.

Row 28: K2, SM, YO, K3, K2 tog, YO, K1, YO, SSK, † K5, K2 tog, YO, K1, YO, SSK †; repeat from † to † across to within 3 sts of center marker, K3, YO, SM, K1, YO, K3, K2 tog, YO, K1, YO, SSK, repeat from † to † across to last 5 sts, K3, YO, SM, K2: 71 sts.

Row 30: K2, SM, YO, K4, K2 tog, YO, K1, YO, SSK, † K5, K2 tog, YO, K1, YO, SSK †; repeat from † to † across to within 4 sts of center marker, K4, YO, SM, K1, YO, K4, K2 tog, YO, K1, YO, SSK, repeat from † to † across to last 6 sts, K4, YO, SM, K2: 75 sts.

Instructions continued on page 41.

KEY

■ No stitch in area	○ Yarn over
| Purl wrong side	╱ K2 tog
— Knit wrong side	I Knit right side
╱ SSK	✳ Center stitch

CHART A

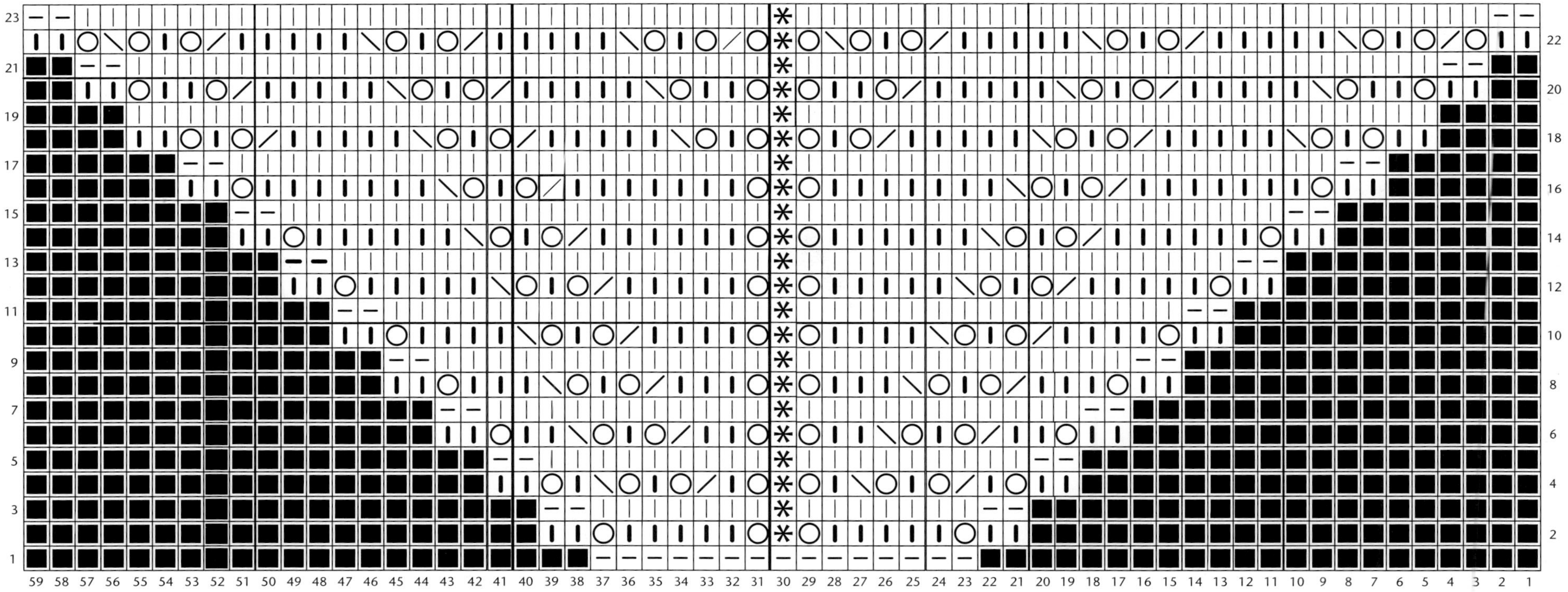

Work from **right** to **left** on **right** side rows; work from **left** to **right** on **wrong** side rows.

Row 32: K2, SM, YO, † K5, K2 tog, YO, K1, YO, SSK †; repeat from † to † across to within 5 sts of center marker, K5, YO, SM, K1, YO, repeat from † to † across to last 7 sts, K5, YO, SM, K2: 79 sts.

Row 34: K2, SM, YO, K6, K2 tog, YO, K1, YO, SSK, † K5, K2 tog, YO, K1, YO, SSK †; repeat from † to † across to within 6 sts of center marker, K6, YO, SM, K1, YO, K6, K2 tog, YO, K1, YO, SSK, repeat from † to † across to last 8 sts, K6, YO, SM, K2: 83 sts.

Row 36: K2, SM, YO, K7, K2 tog, YO, K1, YO, SSK, † K5, K2 tog, YO, K1, YO, SSK †; repeat from † to † across to within 7 sts of center marker, K7, YO, SM, K1, YO, K7, K2 tog, YO, K1, YO, SSK, repeat from † to † across to last 9 sts, K7, YO, SM, K2: 87 sts.

Row 38: K2, SM, YO, K1, YO, SSK, † K5, K2 tog, YO, K1, YO, SSK †; repeat from † to † across to within 8 sts of center marker, K5, K2 tog, YO, K1, YO, SM, (K1, YO) twice, SSK, repeat from † to † across to last 10 sts, K5, K2 tog, YO, K1, YO, SM, K2: 91 sts.

Row 40: K2, SM, YO, K2, YO, SSK, † K5, K2 tog, YO, K1, YO, SSK †; repeat from † to † across to within 9 sts of center marker, K5, K2 tog, YO, K2, YO, SM, K1, YO, K2, YO, SSK, repeat from † to † across to last 11 sts, K5, K2 tog, YO, K2, YO, SM, K2: 95 sts.

Instructions continued on page 42.

Row 42: K2, SM, YO, K2 tog, YO, K1, YO, SSK, † K5, K2 tog, YO, K1, YO, SSK †; repeat from † to † across to within 10 sts of center marker, K5, K2 tog, YO, K1, YO, SSK, YO, SM, K1, YO, K2 tog, YO, K1, YO, SSK, repeat from † to † across to last 2 sts, YO, SM, K2: 99 sts.

Rows 44-115: Repeat Rows 24-43, 3 times; then repeat Rows 24-35 once **more**: 243 sts.

EDGING

Remove all markers when working the next row.

Row 1: K2, YO, SSK, ★ K2 tog, YO, K1, YO, SSK; repeat from ★ across to last 4 sts, K2 tog, YO, K2.

Row 2: K2, purl across to last 2 sts, K2.

Repeat Rows 1 and 2 until Edging measures 3" (7.5 cm), ending by working Row 2.

Working from **left** to **right** on **wrong** side rows, work across Chart C and then work across Chart B.

CHART C

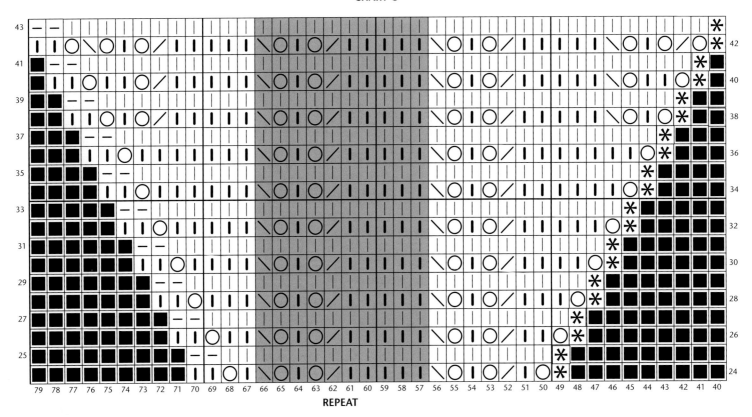

REPEAT

KEY

Center stitch	✱	SSK	╲
No stitch in area	■	Yarn over	○
Purl wrong side	⎮	K2 tog	╱
Knit wrong side	—	Knit right side	⏐

Work the first edge stitches, then repeat the stitches in the shaded area for pattern, ending with working the remaining edge stitches.

Next Row: K2, YO, SSK, ★ YO, K2 tog, YO, K1, YO, SSK; repeat from ★ across to last 4 sts, K2 tog, YO, K2: 290 sts.

Last Row: K2, purl across to last 2 sts, K2.

Bind off all sts as follows: K2, return the 2 sts just worked back on to left needle, K2 tog tbl *(Fig. 4, page 74)*, ★ K1, return the 2 sts on right needle back on to left needle, K2 tog tbl; repeat from ★ across, finish off.

Blocking Instructions: Very gently hand wash Shawl and place on spin cycle in washer to remove excess water. Pin out Shawl on a clean rug to desired blocked dimension. Let dry completely.

Working from **right** to **left** on **right** side rows, work across Chart B and then work across Chart C.

CHART B

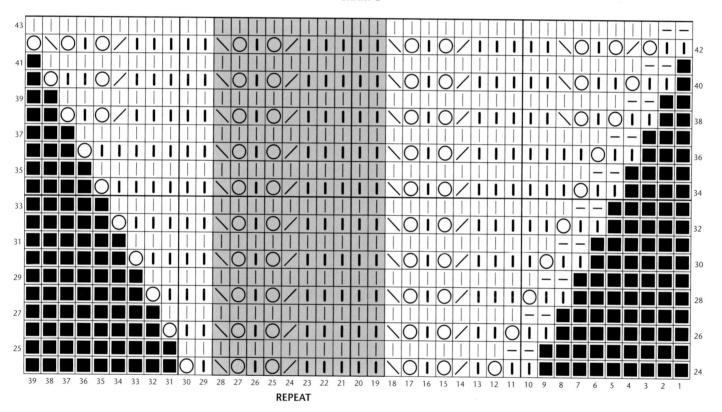

REPEAT

KEY

No stitch in area ■	◯ Yarn over	
Purl wrong side ⏐	╱ K2 tog	
Knit wrong side −	⏐ Knit right side	
SSK ╲		

Work the first edge stitches, then repeat the stitches in the shaded area for pattern, ending with working the remaining edge stitches.

TRIANGULAR *Shawl* 43

LEAF *doily*

 INTERMEDIATE

Finished Size:
   Unblocked - 13¹/₂" (34.5 cm) diameter
   Blocked - 17" (43 cm) diameter

MATERIALS
   Bedspread Weight Cotton Thread
     (size 10): 225 yards (206 meters)
   Double pointed knitting needles, size 3
     (3.25 mm) (set of 4) **or** size needed
     for gauge
   16" (40.5 cm) Circular knitting needle,
     size 3 (3.25 mm)
   Point protector
   Markers

GAUGE: In Stockinette Stitch,
     14 sts = 2"(5 cm)

BODY

Cast 9 sts onto a double pointed needle;
divide 3 sts onto each of 2 other double
pointed needles: 3 sts on **each** needle,
9 sts total.

   Note: Place a marker at the
   first cast on stitch to mark the
   beginning of the round *(see
   Markers, page 73)*. Begin working
   in rounds, making sure that the
   first round is not twisted *(see
   Knitting in the Round, page 73)*.

Rnd 1: Knit around.

When working the next round, do **not** forget to
work the YO at the end of each needle.

Rnd 2: [K1, YO *(Fig. 11a, page 75)*] across each
needle: 6 sts on **each** needle, 18 sts total.

Rnds 3-5: Knit around.

When working the next round, do **not** forget to
work the YO at the end of each needle.

Rnd 6: (K1, YO) across each needle: 12 sts on **each**
needle, 36 sts total.

Rnds 7-12: Knit around.

When working the next round, do **not** forget to
work the YO at the end of each needle.

Rnd 13: (K1, YO) across each needle: 24 sts on **each**
needle, 72 sts total.

Rnd 14: Knit around.

Rnd 15: [K 12, increase *(Figs. 9a & b, page 75)*, K 11]
across each needle: 25 sts on **each** needle, 75 sts total.

Rnd 16: Knit around.

Begin following Chart A, if desired.

KEY		CHART A

Knit — |

SSK — \

Yarn over — O

K2 tog — /

Working from **right** to
left on all rounds, work
across Chart A 5 times
across **each** needle.

Rnd 17: [YO, SSK *(Figs. 5a-c, page 74)*, K2 tog *(Fig. 3, page 73)*, YO, K1] 5 times across each needle.

Rnd 18: Knit around.

Rnds 19-23: Repeat Rnds 17 and 18 twice, then repeat Rnd 17 once **more**.

Rnds 24-26: Knit around.

When working the next round, do **not** forget to work the YO at the end of each needle.

Rnd 27: (K1, YO) across each needle: 50 sts on **each** needle, 150 sts total.

Rnds 28-30: Knit around.

Begin following Chart B, page 46, if desired.

Rnd 31: (YO, K1, YO, SSK, K5, K2 tog) 5 times across **each** needle.

Rnd 32: Knit around.

Rnd 33: (YO, K3, YO, SSK, K3, K2 tog) 5 times across each needle.

Rnd 34: Knit around.

Rnd 35: (YO, K5, YO, SSK, K1, K2 tog) 5 times across each needle.

Rnd 36: Knit around.

Instructions continued on page 46.

Rnd 37: [K7, YO, slip 1, K2 tog, PSSO *(Figs. 6a & b, page 74)*, YO] 5 times across each needle.

Rnd 38: Knit around.

Rnd 39: (K2, slip 1, K2 tog, PSSO, K2, YO, K3, YO) 5 times across each needle.

Rnd 40: Knit around.

Rnd 41: (K1, slip 1, K2 tog, PSSO, K1, YO, K5, YO) 5 times across each needle.

Rnd 42: Knit around.

Rnd 43: (Slip 1, K2 tog, PSSO, YO, K7, YO) 5 times across each needle.

Rnds 44 and 45: Knit around.

When working the next round, replace the double pointed needles with the circular needle.

Rnd 46: (K4, increase) 10 times across each needle: 180 sts total.

Rnds 47 and 48: Knit around.

Cut working yarn; place point protector onto right tip of circular needle.

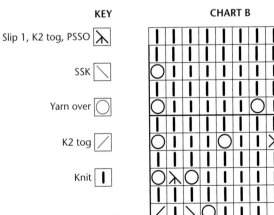

KEY

Slip 1, K2 tog, PSSO   ⋏

SSK   ◺

Yarn over   ○

K2 tog   ◹

Knit |

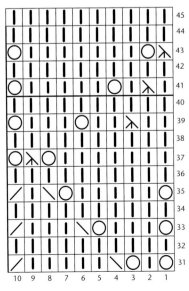

CHART B

Working from **right** to **left** on all rounds, work across Chart B 5 times for **each** needle.

EDGING

With contrasting color of waste thread, cast 19 sts onto left tip of circular needle.

When instructed to slip a stitch, always slip it as if to **knit**.

Foundation Row: With working thread and spare needle, K1, (K2 tog, YO) 3 times, K1, YO, K2, slip 1, K2 tog, PSSO, (K2 tog, YO) twice, K2, knit next st of Body: 19 sts on right needle.

Next Row: Turn; working across Edging sts, K1, K2 tog, YO, K3, P 11, K2.

Begin following Edging Chart, page 47, if desired.

Row 1 (Right side)**:** Slip 1, K1, YO, (K2 tog, YO) twice, K3, YO, SSK, slip 1, K2 tog, PSSO, YO, K2 tog, YO, K2, knit last st of Edging and next st of Body together: 19 sts on right needle.

Row 2: Turn; working across Edging sts, K1, K2 tog, YO, K3, P 11, K2.

Row 3: Slip 1, K1, YO, (K2 tog, YO) twice, K5, YO, slip 1, K2 tog, PSSO, YO, K2 tog, YO, K2, knit last st of Edging and next st of Body together: 20 sts on right needle.

Row 4: Turn; working across Edging sts, K1, K2 tog, YO, K3, P 12, K2.

Row 5: Slip 1, K1, YO, (K2 tog, YO) twice, K7, YO, (K2 tog, YO) twice, K2, knit last st of Edging and next st of Body together: 22 sts on right needle.

Row 6: Turn; working across Edging sts, K1, K2 tog, YO, K3, P 14, K2.

Row 7: Slip 1, K1, YO, (K2 tog, YO) twice, K3, slip 1, K2 tog, PSSO, K3, YO, (K2 tog, YO) twice, K2, knit last st of Edging and next st of Body together: 22 sts on right needle.

Row 8: Turn; working across Edging sts, K1, K2 tog, YO, K3, P 14, K2.

Row 9: Slip 1, (K2 tog, YO) 3 times, K2, slip 1, K2 tog, PSSO, K2, YO, slip 1, K2 tog, PSSO, YO, K2 tog, YO, K2, knit last st of Edging and next st of Body together: 20 sts on right needle.

Row 10: Turn; working across Edging sts, K1, K2 tog, YO, K3, P 12, K2.

Row 11: Slip 1, (K2 tog, YO) 3 times, K1, slip 1, K2 tog, PSSO, K1, YO, K3, YO, K2 tog, YO, K2, knit last st of Edging and next st of Body together: 20 sts on right needle.

Row 12: Turn; working across Edging sts, K1, K2 tog, YO, K3, P 12, K2.

Row 13: Slip 1, (K2 tog, YO) 3 times, slip 1, K2 tog, PSSO, YO, K5, YO, K2 tog, YO, K2, knit last st of Edging and next st of Body together: 20 sts on right needle.

Row 14: Turn; working across Edging sts, K1, K2 tog, YO, K3, P 12, K2.

Row 15: Slip 1, (K2 tog, YO) 3 times, K1, YO, K2, slip 1, K2 tog, PSSO, K2, YO, K2 tog, YO, K2, knit last st of Edging and next st of Body together: 20 sts on right needle.

Row 16: Turn; working across Edging sts, K1, K2 tog, YO, K3, P 12, K2.

Row 17: Slip 1, (K2 tog, YO) 3 times, K1, YO, K2, slip 1, K2 tog, PSSO, (K2 tog, YO) twice, K2, knit last st of Edging and next st of Body together: 19 sts on right needle.

Row 18: Turn; working across Edging sts, K1, K2 tog, YO, K3, P 11, K2.

Repeat Rows 1-18 until all sts of the Body are used, ending by working Row 15.

Carefully matching sts, attach ends of Edging by grafting sts *(Figs. 13a-g, page 76)*. Remove contrasting color waste thread.

Blocking Instructions: Soak Doily in warm water to wet thoroughly. Squeeze out as much water as possible. Place Doily in a bath towel and press firmly to remove excess water. Lay out to blocked dimension, placing a pin in end of Row 7 of each Edging repeat or use blocking wires. Let dry completely.

KEY

No stitch in area ■
Purl wrong side |
Knit wrong side —
Knit Body & Edging st tog ⟀
Slip 1, K2 tog, PSSO ⅄
SSK ╲
Yarn over ○
K2 tog ╱
Knit right side I
Slip 1 S

EDGING CHART

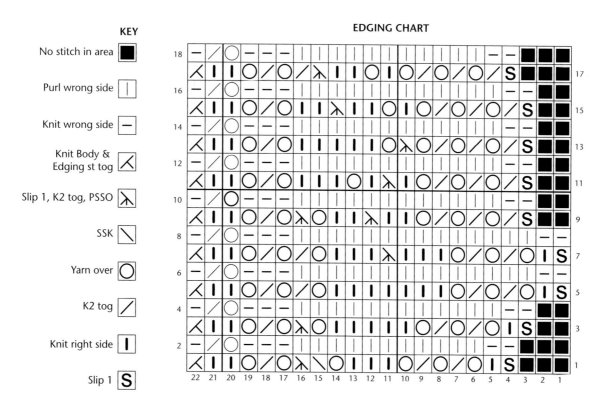

DIAMOND LACE
table topper or shawl

◼◼◼◻ **INTERMEDIATE**

Finished Size:
Unblocked - 55" (139.5 cm) diameter
Blocked - 70" (178 cm) diameter

MATERIALS
Bedspread Weight Cotton Thread,
  (size 10):
  White - 1,800 yards (1,646 meters)
  OR
Ultra Fine Weight Yarn 🔵⓪
  [1.75 ounces, 440 yards
  (50 grams, 402 meters) per hank]:
  Black - 4 hanks (shown on page 54)
Double pointed knitting needles, size 6
  (4 mm) (set of 4) **or** size needed
  for gauge
16" (40.5 cm), 24"(61 cm) **and** 36"
  (91.5 cm) Circular knitting needles,
  size 6 (4 mm)
Markers
Point protector

GAUGE: In Stockinette Stitch,
       24 sts = 4" (10 cm)

BODY
When instructed to slip a stitch,
always slip it as if to **knit**.

Cast 9 sts onto a double pointed needle;
divide 3 sts onto each of 2 other double
pointed needles: 3 sts on **each** needle,
9 sts total.

Note: Place a marker at the first cast on stitch to
mark the beginning of the round *(see Markers,
page 73)*. Begin working in rounds, making sure
that the first round is not twisted *(see Knitting
in the Round, page 73)*.

Rnd 1: Knit around.

When working the next round, do **not** forget to
work the YO at the end of each needle.

Rnd 2: [K1, YO *(Fig. 11a, page 75)*] across each
needle: 6 sts on **each** needle, 18 sts total.

Rnds 3-5: Knit around.

When working the next round, do **not** forget to
work the YO at the end of each needle.

Rnd 6: (K1, YO) across each needle: 12 sts on **each**
needle, 36 sts total.

Rnds 7-12: Knit around.

When working the next round, do **not** forget to
work the YO at the end of each needle.

Rnd 13: (K1, YO) across each needle: 24 sts on **each**
needle, 72 sts total.

Rnds 14-19: Knit around.

Instructions continued on page 50.

Rnd 20: [K 11, increase (*Figs. 9a & b, page 75*), K 12] across each needle: 25 sts on **each** needle, 75 sts total.

Rnds 21-25: Knit around.

At this point, you may be able to replace the double pointed needles with a 16" (40.5 cm) circular needle. When working next round, place markers as indicated, making sure that the beginning marker is a different color/type from all the other markers.

Change to longer circular needles as needed.

Rnd 26: (K1, YO) around placing a marker after every 30 sts: 30 sts in **each** section, 150 sts total.

Rnds 27-31: Knit around.

Begin following Chart A, if desired.

Rnd 32: ★ K5, K2 tog (*Fig. 3, page 73*), YO, K1, YO, SSK (*Figs. 5a-c, page 75*), K 10, K2 tog, YO, K1, YO, SSK, K5; repeat from ★ across each section.

Rnd 33 AND ALL ODD NUMBERED RNDS THRU RND 45: Knit around.

Rnd 34: ★ K4, K2 tog, YO, K3, YO, SSK, K8, K2 tog, YO, K3, YO, SSK, K4; repeat from ★ across each section.

Rnd 36: ★ K3, (K2 tog, YO) twice, K1, (YO, SSK) twice, K6, (K2 tog, YO) twice, K1, (YO, SSK) twice, K3; repeat from ★ across each section.

Rnd 38: ★ K2, (K2 tog, YO) twice, K3, (YO, SSK) twice, K4, (K2 tog, YO) twice, K3, (YO, SSK) twice, K2; repeat from ★ across each section.

CHART A

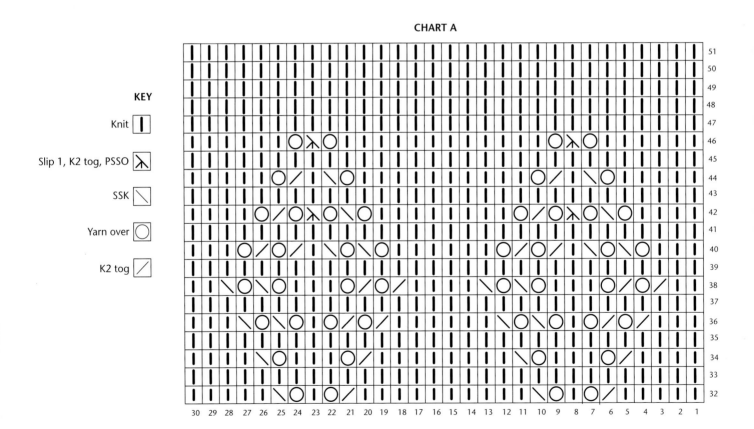

KEY

Knit | |

Slip 1, K2 tog, PSSO | ⋏

SSK | \

Yarn over | O

K2 tog | /

Working from **right** to **left** on all rounds, work Chart A across each section.

Rnd 40: ★ K3, (YO, SSK) twice, K1, (K2 tog, YO) twice, K6, (YO, SSK) twice, K1, (K2 tog, YO) twice, K3; repeat from ★ across each section.

Rnd 42: ★ K4, YO, SSK, YO, [slip 1, K2 tog, PSSO *(Figs. 6a & b, page 74)*], YO, K2 tog, YO, K8, YO, SSK, YO, slip 1, K2 tog, PSSO, YO, K2 tog, YO, K4; repeat from ★ across each section.

Rnd 44: ★ K5, YO, SSK, K1, K2 tog, YO, K 10, YO, SSK, K1, K2 tog, YO, K5; repeat from ★ across each section.

Rnd 46: ★ K6, YO, slip 1, K2 tog, PSSO, YO, K 12, YO, slip 1, K2 tog, PSSO, YO, K6; repeat from ★ across each section.

Rnds 47-51: Knit around.

Rnd 52: (K1, YO) around: 60 sts in **each** section, 300 sts total.

Rnds 53-57: Knit around.

Begin following Chart B, if desired.

Rnd 58: (K1, YO, SSK, K2 tog, YO) around.

Rnd 59 AND ALL ODD NUMBERED RNDS THRU RND 73: Knit around.

Rnd 60: (K1, YO, SSK, K2 tog, YO) around.

Rnd 62: K2, YO, SSK, K3, K2 tog, YO, ★ K3, YO, SSK, K3, K2 tog, YO; repeat from ★ around to last st, K1.

Rnd 64: K3, YO, SSK, K1, K2 tog, YO, ★ K5, YO, SSK, K1, K2 tog, YO; repeat from ★ around to last 2 sts, K2.

Rnd 66: K4, YO, slip 1, K2 tog, PSSO, YO, ★ K7, YO, slip 1, K2 tog, PSSO, YO; repeat from ★ around to last 3 sts, K3.

Rnd 68: K3, K2 tog, YO, K1, YO, SSK, ★ K5, K2 tog, YO, K1, YO, SSK; repeat from ★ around to last 2 sts, K2.

Rnd 70: K2, K2 tog, YO, K3, YO, SSK, ★ K3, K2 tog, YO, K3, YO, SSK; repeat from ★ around to last st, K1.

Instructions continued on page 52.

CHART B

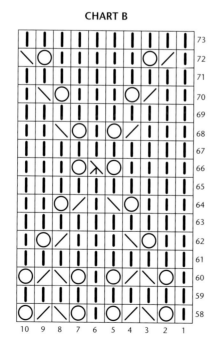

KEY

Knit
Slip 1, K2 tog, PSSO
SSK
Yarn over
K2 tog

Working from **right** to **left** on all rounds, work Chart B 6 times across **each** section.

Rnd 72: (K1, K2 tog, YO, K5, YO, SSK) around.

Rnds 74-92: Repeat Rnds 58-73 once, then repeat Rnds 58-60 once **more**.

Rnds 93-97: Knit around.

Rnd 98: (K1, YO) around, placing additional markers every 60 sts: 60 sts in **each** section, 600 sts total.

Rnds 99-102: Knit around.

Begin following Chart C, if desired.

Rnd 103: ★ (K2 tog, YO) twice, K1, (YO, SSK) twice, K1; repeat from ★ around.

Rnd 104 AND ALL EVEN NUMBERED RNDS THRU RND 114: Knit around.

Rnd 105: K1, K2 tog, YO, K3, YO, SSK, ★ K3, K2 tog, YO, K3, YO, SSK; repeat from ★ around to last 2 sts, K2.

Rnd 107: ★ K2 tog, YO, K5, YO, SSK, K1; repeat from ★ around.

Rnd 109: K1, YO, SSK, K3, K2 tog, YO, ★ K3, YO, SSK, K3, K2 tog, YO; repeat from ★ around to last 2 sts, K2.

Rnd 111: ★ (YO, SSK) twice, K1, (K2 tog, YO) twice, K1; repeat from ★ around.

Rnd 113: K1, YO, SSK, YO, slip 1, K2 tog, PSSO, YO, K2 tog, YO, ★ K3, YO, SSK, YO, slip 1, K2 tog, PSSO, YO, K2 tog, YO; repeat from ★ around to last 2 sts, K2.

Rnds 115-161: Repeat Rnds 103-114, 3 times; then repeat Rnds 103-113 once **more**.

Rnds 162-166: Knit around.

Cut working thread or yarn; place point protector onto right tip of circular needle.

EDGING

With contrasting color of waste thread or yarn, cast 16 sts onto left tip of circular needle.

Foundation Row: With working thread or yarn and spare needle, K1, K2 tog, YO, K1, YO, SSK, K3, K2 tog, YO, K1, K2 tog, YO, K2, knit next st of Body: 17 sts on right needle.

Next Row: Turn; working across Edging sts, K1, K2 tog, YO, K4, P8, K2.

CHART C

KEY

Slip 1, K2 tog, PSSO

SSK

Yarn over

K2 tog

Knit

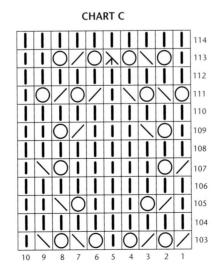

Working from **right** to **left** on all rounds, work Chart C 6 times across **each** section.

Begin following Edging Chart, if desired.

Row 1: Slip 1, K1, YO, K3, YO, SSK, K2, K2 tog, YO, K1, K2 tog, YO, K2, knit last st of Edging and next st of Body together: 18 sts on right needle.

Row 2: Turn; working across Edging sts, K1, K2 tog, YO, K4, P9, K2.

Row 3: Slip 1, K1, YO, K2 tog, YO, K1, (YO, SSK) twice, (K1, K2 tog, YO) twice, K2, knit last st of Edging and next st of Body together: 19 sts on right needle.

Row 4: Turn; working across Edging sts, K1, K2 tog, YO, K4, P 10, K2.

Row 5: Slip 1, K1, YO, K2 tog, YO, K3, (YO, SSK) twice, K2 tog, YO, K1, K2 tog, YO, K2, knit last st of Edging and next st of Body together: 20 sts on right needle.

Row 6: Turn; working across Edging sts, K1, K2 tog, YO, K4, P 11, K2.

Row 7: Slip 1, K1, (YO, SSK) twice, K1, (K2 tog, YO) twice, (K1, K2 tog, YO) twice, K2, knit last st of Edging and next st of Body together: 20 sts on right needle.

Row 8: Turn; working across Edging sts, K1, K2 tog, YO, K4, P 11, K2.

Row 9: Slip 1, (SSK, YO) twice, slip 1, K2 tog, PSSO, YO, K2 tog, YO, K2, K2 tog, YO, K1, K2 tog, YO, K2, knit last st of Edging and next st of Body together: 19 sts on right needle.

Row 10: Turn; working across Edging sts, K1, K2 tog, YO, K4, P 10, K2.

Instructions continued on page 54.

KEY

■	No stitch in area
│	Purl wrong side
—	Knit wrong side
⚟	Knit Body & Edging st tog
⚞	Slip 1, K2 tog, PSSO
\	SSK
○	Yarn over
/	K2 tog
I	Knit right side
S	Slip 1

EDGING CHART

Row 11: Slip 1, SSK, YO, SSK, K1, K2 tog, YO, K3, K2 tog, YO, K1, K2 tog, YO, K2, knit last st of Edging and next st of Body together: 18 sts on right needle.

Row 12: Turn; working across Edging sts, K1, K2 tog, YO, K4, P9, K2.

Row 13: Slip 1, SSK, YO, slip 1, K2 tog, PSSO, YO, K4, K2 tog, YO, K1, K2 tog, YO, K2, knit last st of Edging and next st of Body together: 17 sts on right needle.

Row 14: Turn; working across Edging sts, K1, K2 tog, YO, K4, P8, K2.

Row 15: Slip 1, K2 tog, YO, K1, YO, SSK, K3, K2 tog, YO, K1, K2 tog, YO, K2, knit last st of Edging and next st of Body together: 17 sts on right needle.

Row 16: Turn; working across Edging sts, K1, K2 tog, YO, K4, P8, K2.

Repeat Rows 1-16 until all sts of the Body are used, ending by working Row 13.

Carefully matching sts, attach ends of Edging by grafting sts *(Figs. 13a-g, page 76)*. Remove contrasting color waste thread or yarn.

Blocking Instructions: Hand wash in mild dish soap. Rinse very gently. Place on spin cycle in washer to remove excess water. Lay out wet Table Topper/Shawl to blocked dimension, pin in place. Let dry completely.

SAMPLER *scarf*

Instructions begin on page 56.

SAMPLER *scarf*

Shown on page 55.

Note: The Scarf is worked in panels of pattern stitches with a top and a bottom edging.

■■■□ **INTERMEDIATE**

Finished Size:
 Unblocked - 6$\frac{1}{4}$"w x 63"h (16 cm x 160 cm)
 Blocked - 7$\frac{3}{4}$"w x 78"h (19.5 cm x 198 cm)

MATERIALS
 Fingering/Sock Weight Yarn **SUPER FINE 1**
 [1.75 ounces, 203 yards
 (50 grams, 187 meters) per ball]:
  2 balls
 Straight knitting needles, size 7 (4.5 mm) **or** size
  needed for gauge
 Markers

GAUGE: In Stockinette Stitch,
  20 sts and 26 rows = 4" (10 cm)

Remember that the Scarf will stretch approximately 20-30% when blocked.

When instructed to slip a stitch, always slip it as if to **knit**.

TOP EYELET DIAMOND EDGING

Cast on 17 sts.

Foundation Row: K7, purl across to last 2 sts, K2.

Begin following Top Eyelet Diamond Edging Chart, page 57, if desired.

Row 1 (Right side)**:** Slip 1, K2 tog (*Fig. 3, page 73*), YO (*Fig. 11a, page 75*), K1, YO, SSK (*Figs. 5a-c, page 74*), K3, K2 tog, YO, K1, K2 tog, YO, K3.

Row 2: Slip 1, K2 tog, YO, K4, P8, K2.

Row 3: Slip 1, K1, YO, K3, YO, SSK, K2, K2 tog, YO, K1, K2 tog, YO, K3: 18 sts.

Row 4: Slip 1, K2 tog, YO, K4, P9, K2.

Row 5: Slip 1, K1, YO, K2 tog, YO, K1, (YO, SSK) twice, (K1, K2 tog, YO) twice, K3: 19 sts.

Row 6: Slip 1, K2 tog, YO, K4, P 10, K2.

Row 7: Slip 1, K1, YO, K2 tog, YO, K3, (YO, SSK) twice, K2 tog, YO, K1, K2 tog, YO, K3: 20 sts.

Row 8: Slip 1, K2 tog, YO, K4, P 11, K2.

Row 9: Slip 1, K1, (YO, SSK) twice, K1, (K2 tog, YO) twice, (K1, K2 tog, YO) twice, K3.

Row 10: Slip 1, K2 tog, YO, K4, P 11, K2.

Row 11: Slip 1, (SSK, YO) twice, [slip 1, K2 tog, PSSO (*Figs. 6a & b, page 74*)], YO, K2 tog, YO, K2, K2 tog, YO, K1, K2 tog, YO, K3: 19 sts.

Row 12: Slip 1, K2 tog, YO, K4, P 10, K2.

Row 13: Slip 1, SSK, YO, SSK, K1, K2 tog, YO, K3, K2 tog, YO, K1, K2 tog, YO, K3: 18 sts.

Row 14: Slip 1, K2 tog, YO, K4, P9, K2.

Row 15: Slip 1, SSK, YO, slip 1, K2 tog, PSSO, YO, K4, K2 tog, YO, K1, K2 tog, YO, K3: 17 sts.

Row 16: Slip 1, K2 tog, YO, K4, P8, K2.

Repeat Rows 1-16 twice.

Bind off all sts in **knit**; leaving last st on needle.

BODY

With **right** side of Edging facing, pick up 30 sts evenly spaced across end of rows (*Fig. 12, page 75*): 31 sts.

Row 1: K4, P2, place marker (*see Markers, page 73*), purl across to last 5 sts, place marker, P1, K4.

Row 2: Slip 1, K1, K2 tog, YO, knit across to last marker, K2, K2 tog, YO, K2.

Row 3: Slip 1, K1, K2 tog, YO (*Fig. 11b, page 75*), purl across to last marker, P1, K2 tog, YO, K2.

Row 4: Slip 1, K1, K2 tog, YO, knit across to last marker, K2, K2 tog, YO, K2.

Row 5: Slip 1, K1, K2 tog, YO, purl across to last marker, P1, K2 tog, YO, K2.

Instructions continued on page 58.

KEY

■	No stitch in area
|	Purl wrong side
—	Knit wrong side
人	Slip 1, K2 tog, PSSO
\	SSK
O	Yarn over
/	K2 tog
I	Knit right side
S	Slip 1

TOP EYELET DIAMOND EDGING CHART

Column numbers (right to left): 20 19 18 17 16 15 14 13 12 11 10 9 8 7 6 5 4 3 2 1

Row numbers: 1–16

LADDER STITCH PANEL

Begin following Ladder Stitch Panel Chart, if desired.

Row 1: Slip 1, K1, K2 tog, YO, K2, YO, SSK, K2 tog, YO, (K1, YO, SSK, K2 tog, YO) across to last marker, K2, K2 tog, YO, K2.

Row 2: Slip 1, K1, K2 tog, YO, purl across to last marker, P1, K2 tog, YO, K2.

Rows 3-8: Repeat Rows 1 and 2, 3 times.

Row 9: Slip 1, K1, K2 tog, YO, knit across to last marker, K2, K2 tog, YO, K2.

Row 10: Slip 1, K1, K2 tog, YO, purl across to last marker, P1, K2 tog, YO, K2.

Rows 11 and 12: Repeat Rows 9 and 10.

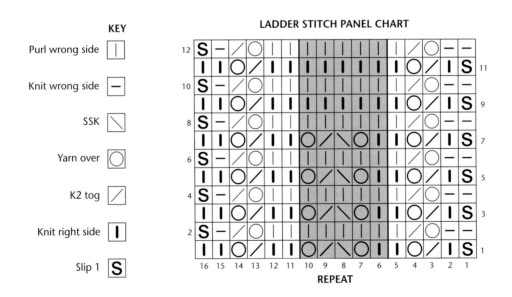

KEY

Purl wrong side

Knit wrong side

SSK

Yarn over

K2 tog

Knit right side

Slip 1

LADDER STITCH PANEL CHART

REPEAT

Work the first edge stitches, then repeat the stitches in the shaded area for pattern, ending with working the remaining edge stitches.

HORSESHOE STITCH PANEL

Begin following Horseshoe Stitch Panel Chart, if desired.

Row 1: Slip 1, K1, K2 tog, YO, K2, YO, K3, slip 1, K2 tog, PSSO, K3, YO, K1, YO, K3, slip 1, K2 tog, PSSO, K3, YO, K2, K2 tog, YO, K2.

Row 2 AND ALL WRONG SIDE ROWS: Slip 1, K1, K2 tog, YO, purl across to last marker, P1, K2 tog, YO, K2.

Row 3: Slip 1, K1, K2 tog, YO, K3, ★ YO, K2, slip 1, K2 tog, PSSO, K2, YO, K3; repeat from ★ once **more**, K2 tog, YO, K2.

Row 5: Slip 1, K1, K2 tog, YO, K4, YO, K1, slip 1, K2 tog, PSSO, K1, YO, K5, YO, K1, slip 1, K2 tog, PSSO, K1, YO, K4, K2 tog, YO, K2.

Row 7: Slip 1, K1, K2 tog, YO, K5, YO, slip 1, K2 tog, PSSO, YO, K7, YO, slip 1, K2 tog, PSSO, YO, K5, K2 tog, YO, K2.

Row 9: Slip 1, K1, K2 tog, YO, knit across to last marker, K2, K2 tog, YO, K2.

Rows 11 and 12: Repeat Rows 9 and 10.

Instructions continued on page 60.

KEY

Purl wrong side	[I]
Knit wrong side	[—]
Slip 1, K2 tog, PSSO	[⋏]
Yarn over	[O]
K2 tog	[/]
Knit right side	[I]
Slip 1	[S]

HORSESHOE STITCH PANEL CHART

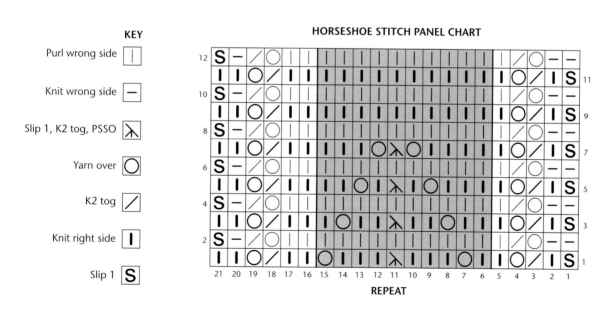

REPEAT

Work the first edge stitches, then repeat the stitches in the shaded area for pattern, ending with working the remaining edge stitches.

CHEVRON & OPEN RIB PANEL

Begin following Chevron and Open Rib Panel Chart, if desired.

Row 1: Slip 1, K1, K2 tog, YO, K2, (K2 tog, YO) twice, K1, (YO, SSK) twice, K1, (K2 tog, YO) twice, K1, (YO, SSK) twice, K2, K2 tog, YO, K2.

Row 2: Slip 1, K1, K2 tog, YO, purl across to last marker, P1, K2 tog, YO, K2.

Rows 3-8: Repeat Rows 1 and 2, 3 times.

Row 9: Slip 1, K1, K2 tog, YO, knit across to last marker, K2, K2 tog, YO, K2.

Row 10: Slip 1, K1, K2 tog, YO, purl across to last marker, P1, K2 tog, YO, K2.

Rows 11 and 12: Repeat Rows 9 and 10.

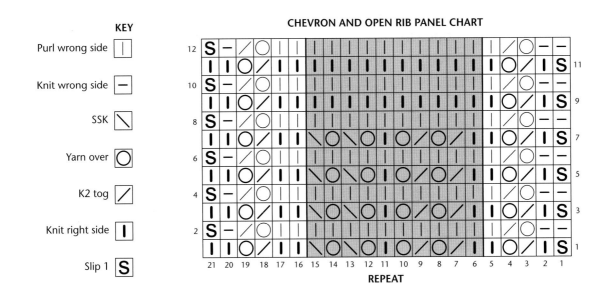

CHEVRON AND OPEN RIB PANEL CHART

KEY

Purl wrong side

Knit wrong side

SSK

Yarn over

K2 tog

Knit right side

Slip 1

Work the first edge stitches, then repeat the stitches in the shaded area for pattern, ending with working the remaining edge stitches.

DIAMOND LATTICE PANEL

Begin following Diamond Lattice Panel Chart, page 62, if desired.

Row 1: Slip 1, K1, K2 tog, YO, K2, YO, SSK, K2 tog, YO, (K1, YO, SSK, K2 tog, YO) across to last marker, K2, K2 tog, YO, K2.

Row 2 AND ALL WRONG SIDE ROWS: Slip 1, K1, K2 tog, YO, purl across to last marker, P1, K2 tog, YO, K2.

Row 3: Slip 1, K1, K2 tog, YO, K2, YO, SSK, K2 tog, YO, (K1, YO, SSK, K2 tog, YO) across to last marker, K2, K2 tog, YO, K2.

Row 5: Slip 1, K1, K2 tog, YO, K3, ★ YO, SSK, K3, K2 tog, YO, K3; repeat from ★ once **more**, K2 tog, YO, K2.

Row 7: Slip 1, K1, K2 tog, YO, K4, YO, SSK, K1, K2 tog, YO, K5, YO, SSK, K1, K2 tog, YO, K4, K2 tog, YO, K2.

Row 9: Slip 1, K1, K2 tog, YO, K5, YO, slip 1, K2 tog, PSSO, YO, K7, YO, slip 1, K2 tog, PSSO, YO, K5, K2 tog, YO, K2.

Row 11: Slip 1, K1, K2 tog, YO, K4, K2 tog, YO, K1, YO, SSK, K5, K2 tog, YO, K1, YO, SSK, K4, K2 tog, YO, K2.

Row 13: Slip 1, K1, K2 tog, YO, K3, ★ K2 tog, YO, K3, YO, SSK, K3; repeat from ★ once **more**, K2 tog, YO, K2.

Row 15: Slip 1, K1, K2 tog, YO, K2, K2 tog, YO, K5, YO, SSK, K1, K2 tog, YO, K5, YO, SSK, K2, K2 tog, YO, K2.

Rows 17-20: Repeat Rows 1-4.

Row 21: Slip 1, K1, K2 tog, YO, knit across to last marker, K2, K2 tog, YO, K2.

Rows 23 and 24: Repeat Rows 21 and 22.

LADDER STITCH PANEL
Rows 1-22: Repeat Rows 1 and 2 of Ladder Stitch Panel, page 58, 11 times.

Rows 23-26: Repeat Rows 9-12 of Ladder Stitch Panel.

HORSESHOE STITCH PANEL
Rows 1-24: Repeat Rows 1-8 of Horseshoe Stitch Panel, page 59, 3 times.

Rows 25-28: Repeat Rows 9-12 of Horseshoe Stitch Panel.

DIAMOND LATTICE PANEL
Rows 1-36: Repeat Rows 1-16 of Diamond Lattice Panel twice; then repeat Rows 1-4 once **more**.

Rows 37-40: Repeat Rows 21-24 of Diamond Lattice Panel.

Instructions continued on page 62.

KEY

Purl wrong side | |
Knit wrong side —
Slip 1, K2 tog, PSSO ⅄
SSK ＼
Yarn over ○
K2 tog ／
Knit right side |
Slip 1 S

Row numbers (right side, odd): 1, 3, 5, 7, 9, 11, 13, 15, 17, 19, 21, 23
Row numbers (left side, even): 2, 4, 6, 8, 10, 12, 14, 16, 18, 20, 22, 24

Column numbers (bottom): 21 20 19 18 17 16 15 14 13 12 11 10 9 8 7 6 5 4 3 2 1

REPEAT

Work the first edge stitches, then repeat the stitches in the shaded area for pattern, ending with working the remaining edge stitches.

PINECONE STITCH PANEL

Begin following Pinecone Stitch Panel Chart, page 63, if desired.

Row 1: Slip 1, K1, K2 tog, YO, K2, SSK, K2, YO, K1, YO, K2, K2 tog, K1, SSK, K2, YO, K1, YO, K2, K2 tog, K2, K2 tog, YO, K2.

Row 2: Slip 1, K1, K2 tog, YO, purl across to last marker, P1, K2 tog, YO, K2.

Rows 3-6: Repeat Rows 1 and 2 twice.

Row 7: Slip 1, K1, K2 tog, YO, K2, YO, SSK, K5, K2 tog, YO, K1, YO, SSK, K5, K2 tog, YO, K2, K2 tog, YO, K2.

Row 8: Slip 1, K1, K2 tog, YO, purl across to last marker, P1, K2 tog, YO, K2.

Row 9: Slip 1, K1, K2 tog, YO, K3, ★ YO, SSK, K3, K2 tog, YO, K3; repeat from ★ once **more**, K2 tog, YO, K2.

Row 10: Slip 1, K1, K2 tog, YO, purl across to last marker, P1, K2 tog, YO, K2.

Row 11: Slip 1, K1, K2 tog, YO, K4, YO, SSK, K1, K2 tog, YO, K5, YO, SSK, K1, K2 tog, YO, K4, K2 tog, YO, K2.

Row 12: Slip 1, K1, K2 tog, YO, purl across to last marker, P1, K2 tog, YO, K2.

Row 13: Slip 1, K1, K2 tog, (YO, K2) twice, K2 tog, K1, SSK, K2, YO, K1, YO, K2, K2 tog, K1, SSK, K2, YO, K2, K2 tog, YO, K2.

Row 14: Slip 1, K1, K2 tog, YO, purl across to last marker, P1, K2 tog, YO, K2.

Rows 15-18: Repeat Rows 13 and 14 twice.

Row 19: Slip 1, K1, K2 tog, YO, K4, K2 tog, YO, K1, YO, SSK, K5, K2 tog, YO, K1, YO, SSK, K4, K2 tog, YO, K2.

Row 20: Slip 1, K1, K2 tog, YO, purl across to last marker, P1, K2 tog, YO, K2.

Row 21: Slip 1, K1, K2 tog, YO, K3, K2 tog, ★ YO, K3, YO, SSK, K3, K2 tog, repeat from ★ once **more**, YO, K2.

Row 22: Slip 1, K1, K2 tog, YO, purl across to last marker, P1, K2 tog, YO, K2.

Row 23: Slip 1, K1, K2 tog, YO, K2, K2 tog, YO, K5, YO, SSK, K1, K2 tog, YO, K5, YO, SSK, K2, K2 tog, YO, K2.

Row 24: Slip 1, K1, K2 tog, YO, purl across to last marker, P1, K2 tog, YO, K2.

Rows 25-54: Repeat Rows 1-24 once; then repeat Rows 1-6 once **more**.

Row 55: Slip 1, K1, K2 tog, YO, knit across to last marker, K2, K2 tog, YO, K2.

Row 56: Slip 1, K1, K2 tog, YO, purl across to last marker, P1, K2 tog, YO, K2.

Rows 57 and 58: Repeat Rows 55 and 56.

Instructions continued on page 64.

PINECONE STITCH PANEL CHART

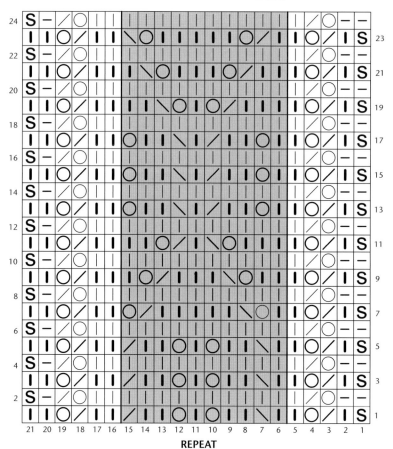

REPEAT

KEY

		Purl wrong side
---	Knit wrong side
\	SSK
O	Yarn over
/	K2 tog
I	Knit right side
S	Slip 1

Work the first edge stitches, then repeat the stitches in the shaded area for pattern, ending with working the remaining edge stitches.

DIAMOND LATTICE PANEL

Rows 1-36: Repeat Rows 1-16 of Diamond Lattice Panel, page 61, twice; then repeat Rows 1-4 once **more**.

Rows 37-40: Repeat Rows 21-24 of Diamond Lattice Panel.

HORSESHOE STITCH PANEL

Rows 1-24: Repeat Rows 1-8 of Horseshoe Stitch Panel, page 59, 3 times.

Rows 25-28: Repeat Rows 9-12 of Horseshoe Stitch Panel.

LADDER STITCH PANEL

Rows 1-22: Repeat Rows 1 and 2 of Ladder Stitch Panel, page 58, 11 times.

Rows 23-26: Repeat Rows 9-12 of Ladder Stitch Panel.

DIAMOND LATTICE PANEL

Rows 1-24: Repeat Rows 1-24 of Diamond Lattice Panel, page 61.

CHEVRON AND OPEN RIB PANEL

Rows 1-12: Repeat Rows 1-12 of Chevron and Open Rib Panel, page 60.

HORSESHOE STITCH PANEL

Rows 1-12: Repeat Rows 1-12 of Horseshoe Stitch Panel, page 59.

LADDER STITCH PANEL

Rows 1-11: Repeat Rows 1-11 of Ladder Stitch Panel, page 58.

When working the next row, remove all markers.

Last Row: K2, K2 tog, [P2, P2 tog *(Fig. 7, page 74)*] across to last 7 sts, P3, K2 tog, K2: 24 sts.

BOTTOM EYELET DIAMOND EDGING

EDGING

Add 17 sts onto working needle *(Figs. 10a & b, page 75)*.

Begin following Bottom Eyelet Diamond Edging Chart, page 65, if desired.

Row 1: Slip 1, K2 tog, YO, K1, YO, SSK, K3, K2 tog, YO, K1, K2 tog, YO, K2, knit last st of Edging and next st of Body together, leave remaining sts unworked: 17 sts on right needle.

Row 2: Turn; working across Edging sts, K1, K2 tog, YO, K4, P8, K2.

Row 3: Slip 1, K1, YO, K3, YO, SSK, K2, K2 tog, YO, K1, K2 tog, YO, K2, knit last st of Edging and next st of Body together, leave remaining sts unworked: 18 sts on right needle.

Row 4: Turn; working across Edging sts, K1, K2 tog, YO, K4, P9, K2.

Row 5: Slip 1, K1, YO, K2 tog, YO, K1, (YO, SSK) twice, (K1, K2 tog, YO) twice, K2, knit last st of Edging and next st of Body together, leave remaining sts unworked: 19 sts on right needle.

Row 6: Turn; working across Edging sts, K1, K2 tog, YO, K4, P 10, K2.

Row 7: Slip 1, K1, YO, K2 tog, YO, K3, (YO, SSK) twice, K2 tog, YO, K1, K2 tog, YO, K2, knit last st of Edging and next st of Body together, leave remaining sts unworked: 20 sts on right needle.

Row 8: Turn; working across Edging sts, K1, K2 tog, YO, K4, P 11, K2.

Row 9: Slip 1, K1, (YO, SSK) twice, K1, (K2 tog, YO) twice, (K1, K2 tog, YO) twice, K2, knit last st of Edging and next st of Body together, leave remaining sts unworked: 20 sts on right needle.

Row 10: Turn; working across Edging sts, K1, K2 tog, YO, K4, P 11, K2.

Row 11: Slip 1, (SSK, YO) twice, slip 1, K2 tog, PSSO, YO, K2 tog, YO, K2, K2 tog, YO, K1, K2 tog, YO, K2, knit last st of Edging and next st of Body together, leave remaining sts unworked: 19 sts on right needle.

Row 12: Turn; working across Edging sts, K1, K2 tog, YO, K4, P 10, K2.

Row 13: Slip 1, SSK, YO, SSK, K1, K2 tog, YO, K3, K2 tog, YO, K1, K2 tog, YO, K2, knit last st of Edging and next st of Body together, leave remaining sts unworked: 18 sts on right needle.

Row 14: Turn; working across Edging sts, K1, K2 tog, YO, K4, P9, K2.

Row 15: Slip 1, SSK, YO, slip 1, K2 tog, PSSO, YO, K4, K2 tog, YO, K1, K2 tog, YO, K2, knit last st of Edging and next st of Body together, leave remaining sts unworked: 17 sts on right needle.

Row 16: Turn; working across Edging sts, K1, K2 tog, YO, K4, P8, K2.

Repeat Rows 1-16 until all sts of the Body are used, ending by working Row 15.

Bind off all sts in **knit**.

Care and Blocking Instructions: Gently hand wash Scarf and place on spin cycle in washer to remove excess water. Pin out Scarf to desired blocked dimensions. Let dry completely.

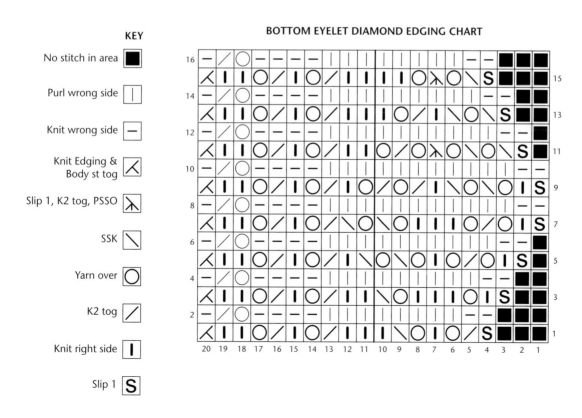

KEY

No stitch in area ■

Purl wrong side

Knit wrong side —

Knit Edging & Body st tog

Slip 1, K2 tog, PSSO

SSK \

Yarn over O

K2 tog /

Knit right side I

Slip 1 S

BOTTOM EYELET DIAMOND EDGING CHART

⬤⬤⬤◻ INTERMEDIATE

Finished Size:
Unblocked - 46" (117 cm) square
Blocked - 58" (147.5 cm) square

MATERIALS
Light Weight Yarn [FINE 2]
[1.75 ounces, 200 yards
(50 grams, 182 meters) per ball]:
Blue - 4 balls (shown on page 69)
OR
Ultra Fine Weight Yarn [LACE 0]
(3 ounces, 1,460 yards
(100 grams, 1,335 meters) per hank]:
Red **or** Brown - 2 hanks
(Brown shown on page 71)
Note: Ultra Fine Weight Yarn is used
holding two strands together
throughout.
Double pointed knitting needles,
size 7 (4.5 mm) (set of 5) **or** size
needed for gauge
16" (40.5 cm), 24" (61 cm) **and** 36"
(91.5 cm) Circular knitting needles,
size 7 (4.5 mm)
Markers

GAUGE: In Stockinette Stitch,
20 sts = 4" (10 cm)

Chart A shows one-fourth of the stitches on
Rnds 1-17. Work across Chart A for all needles
(sections), working from **right** to **left** on all
rounds.

Cast 12 sts onto a double pointed needle; divide 3 sts
onto each of 3 other double pointed needles: 3 sts on
each needle, 12 sts total.

Note: Place a marker at the first cast on stitch to
mark the beginning of the round (*see Markers,
page 73*). Begin working in rounds, making sure
that the first round is not twisted (*see Knitting
in the Round, page 73*).

Begin following Chart A, if desired.

Rnd 1 AND ALL ODD NUMBERED RNDS: Knit
around.

Rnd 2: ★ K1, [YO (*Fig. 11a, page 75*), K1] twice;
repeat from ★ across each needle: 5 sts on **each**
needle, 20 sts total.

Instructions continued on page 68.

CHART A

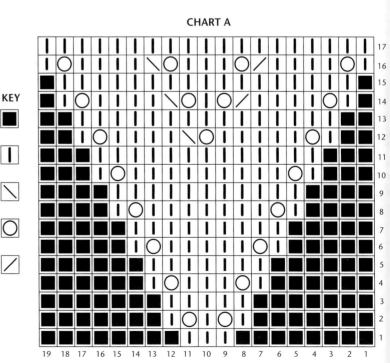

KEY

No stitch in area ◼
Knit |
SSK ╲
Yarn over ◯
K2 tog ╱

Rnd 4: (K1, YO, K3, YO, K1) across each needle: 7 sts on **each** needle, 28 sts total.

Rnd 6: (K1, YO, K5, YO, K1) across each needle: 9 sts on **each** needle, 36 sts total.

Rnd 8: (K1, YO, K7, YO, K1) across each needle: 11 sts on **each** needle, 44 sts total.

Rnd 10: (K1, YO, K9, YO, K1) across each needle: 13 sts on **each** needle, 52 sts total.

Rnd 12: ★ K1, YO, K5, YO, SSK *(Figs. 5a-c, page 74)*, K4, YO, K1; repeat from ★ across each needle: 15 sts on **each** needle, 60 sts total.

Rnd 14: ★ K1, YO, K4, K2 tog *(Fig. 3, page 73)*, YO, K1, YO, SSK, K4, YO, K1; repeat from ★ across each needle: 17 sts on **each** needle, 68 sts total.

Rnd 16: ★ K1, YO, K4, K2 tog, YO, K3, YO, SSK, K4, YO, K1; repeat from ★ across each needle: 19 sts on **each** needle, 76 sts total.

At this point you may be able to replace the double pointed needles with a 16" (40.5 cm) circular needle. Place markers between each section of stitches. Instructions will now reflect that change by working across each section. Use a different color/type marker to mark the beginning of the round.

Change to longer circular needles as needed.

Begin following Chart B, page 70, if desired.

Rnd 18: ★ K1, YO, K2 tog, YO, K1, YO, SSK, (K7, K2 tog, YO, K1, YO, SSK) across to within one st of next marker, YO, K1; repeat from ★ across each section: 21 sts in **each** section, 84 sts total.

Rnd 20: ★ K1, YO, K1, K2 tog, YO, K1, YO, SSK, (K3, YO, SSK, K2, K2 tog, YO, K1, YO, SSK) across to within 2 sts of next marker, K1, YO, K1; repeat from ★ across each section: 23 sts in **each** section, 92 sts total.

Rnd 22: ★ K1, YO, K2, K2 tog, YO, K1, YO, SSK, (K1, K2 tog, YO, K1, YO, SSK) across to within 3 sts of next marker, K2, YO, K1; repeat from ★ across each section: 25 sts in **each** section, 100 sts total.

Rnd 24: ★ K1, YO, K3, K2 tog, YO, K1, YO, SSK, (K2 tog, YO, K3, YO, SSK, K2 tog, YO, K1, YO, SSK) across to within 4 sts of next marker, K3, YO, K1; repeat from ★ across each section: 27 sts in **each** section, 108 sts total.

Rnd 26: ★ K1, YO, K4, K2 tog, YO, K1, YO, SSK, (K7, K2 tog, YO, K1, YO, SSK) across to within 5 sts of next marker, K4, YO, K1; repeat from ★ across each section: 29 sts in **each** section, 116 sts total.

Rnd 28: ★ K1, YO, K5, K2 tog, YO, K1, YO, SSK, (K3, YO, SSK, K2, K2 tog, YO, K1, YO, SSK) across to within 6 sts of next marker, K5, YO, K1; repeat from ★ across each section: 31 sts in **each** section, 124 sts total.

Rnd 30: ★ K1, YO, K6, K2 tog, YO, K1, YO, SSK, (K1, K2 tog, YO, K1, YO, SSK) across to within 7 sts of next marker, K6, YO, K1; repeat from ★ across each section: 33 sts in **each** section, 132 sts total.

Rnd 32: ★ K1, YO, K7, K2 tog, YO, K1, YO, SSK, (K2 tog, YO, K3, YO, SSK, K2 tog, YO, K1, YO, SSK) across to within 8 sts of next marker, K7, YO, K1; repeat from ★ across each section: 35 sts in **each** section, 140 sts total.

Rnd 34: ★ K1, YO, K8, K2 tog, YO, K1, YO, SSK, (K7, K2 tog, YO, K1, YO, SSK) across to within 9 sts of next marker, K8, YO, K1; repeat from ★ across each section: 37 sts in **each** section, 148 sts total.

Instructions continued on page 70.

Rnd 36: ★ K1, YO, K5, YO, SSK, (K2, K2 tog, YO, K1, YO, SSK, K3, YO, SSK) across to within 5 sts of next marker, K4, YO, K1; repeat from ★ across each section: 39 sts in **each** section, 156 sts total.

Rnd 38: ★ K1, YO, K4, K2 tog, YO, K1, YO, SSK, (K1, K2 tog, YO, K1, YO, SSK) across to within 5 sts of next marker, K4, YO, K1; repeat from ★ across each section: 41 sts in **each** section, 164 sts total.

Rnd 40: ★ K1, YO, K4, K2 tog, YO, K3, YO, SSK, (K2 tog, YO, K1, YO, SSK, K2 tog, YO, K3, YO, SSK) across to within 5 sts of next marker, K4, YO, K1; repeat from ★ across each section: 43 sts in **each** section, 172 sts total.

Rnds 42-161: Repeat Rows 18-41, 5 times: 163 sts in **each** section, 652 sts total.

CHART B

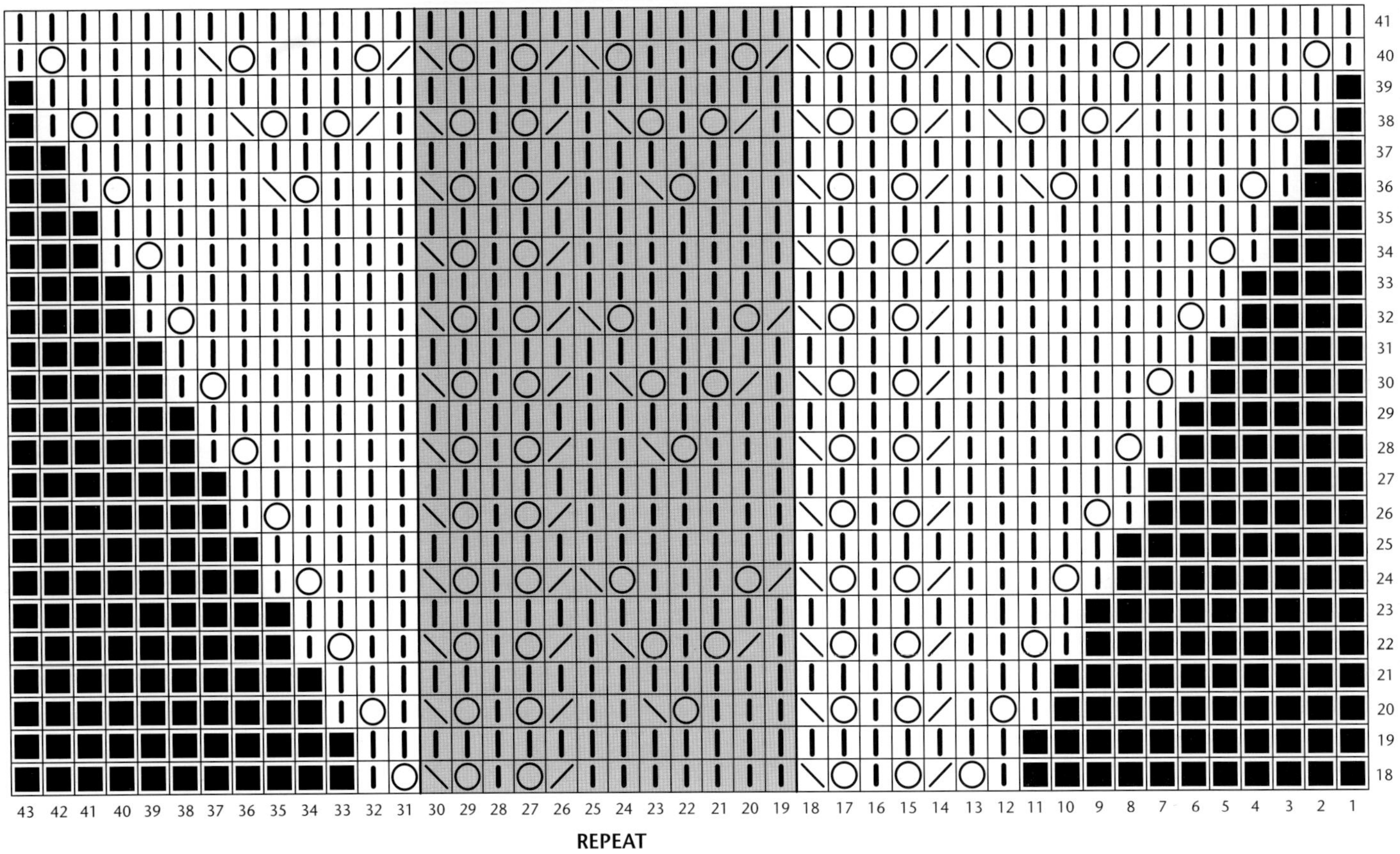

REPEAT

KEY

No stitch in area	■
Knit	I
SSK	\
Yarn over	O
K2 tog	/

Chart B shows one-fourth of the stitches on Rnds 18-41. Work across Chart B for all sections, working from **right** to **left** on all rounds. Work the beginning stitches, then repeat the stitches in the shaded area for pattern, ending with working the end stitches.

Rnd 162: ★ YO, [slip 1, K2 tog, PSSO *(Figs. 6a & b, page 74)*], YO, K1, YO, (SSK, K2 tog, YO, slip 1, K2 tog, PSSO, YO, SSK, K2 tog, YO, K1, YO) across to within 3 sts of next marker, slip 1, K2 tog, PSSO; repeat from ★ across each section: 136 sts in **each** section, 544 sts total.

Double increases are made by working (K1, P1, K1) **all** in the same stitch. Double increases will always be worked in the YO's of the previous round.

Rnd 163: ★ Work double increase, (K1, work double increase) twice, (K2 tog, work double increase, K1, work double increase) across to within one st of next marker, K1; repeat from ★ across each section: 220 sts in **each** section, 880 sts total.

Bind off all sts in K1, P1 rib.

Blocking Instructions: Hand wash in mild dish soap. Rinse very gently. Place on spin cycle in washer to remove excess water. Lay out damp Shawl to blocked dimension, placing a pin in each space below the double increases worked on the last round to form a scalloped edge. If using blocking wires, insert the wire in each space below the double increases worked on the last round. Let dry completely.

GENERAL *instructions*

ABBREVIATIONS

cm	centimeters
K	knit
mm	millimeters
P	purl
PSSO	pass slipped stitch over
Rnd(s)	Round(s)
SM	slip marker
SSK	slip, slip, knit
st(s)	stitch(es)
tbl	through back loop(s)
tog	together
YO	yarn over

★ — work instructions following ★ as many **more** times as indicated in addition to the first time.

† to † — work all instructions from first † to second † **as many** times as specified.

KNIT TERMINOLOGY	
UNITED STATES	**INTERNATIONAL**
gauge =	tension
bind off =	cast off
yarn over (YO) =	yarn forward (yfwd) **or**
	yarn around needle (yrn)

( ) or [ ] — work enclosed instructions **as many** times as specified by the number immediately following **or** work all enclosed instructions in the stitch or space indicated **or** contains explanatory remarks.

colon (:) — the number(s) given after a colon at the end of a row or round denote(s) the number of stitches you should have on that row or round.

work even — work without increasing or decreasing in the established pattern.

Yarn Weight Symbol & Names	LACE 0	SUPER FINE 1	FINE 2	LIGHT 3	MEDIUM 4	BULKY 5	SUPER BULKY 6
Type of Yarns in Category	Fingering, size 10 crochet thread	Sock, Fingering, Baby	Sport, Baby	DK, Light Worsted	Worsted, Afghan, Aran	Chunky, Craft, Rug	Bulky, Roving
Knit Gauge Range* in Stockinette St to 4" (10 cm)	33-40** sts	27-32 sts	23-26 sts	21-24 sts	16-20 sts	12-15 sts	6-11 sts
Advised Needle Size Range	000-1	1 to 3	3 to 5	5 to 7	7 to 9	9 to 11	11 and larger

*GUIDELINES ONLY: The chart above reflects the most commonly used gauges and needle sizes for specific yarn categories.

** Lace weight yarns are usually knitted on larger needles to create lacy openwork patterns. Accordingly, a gauge range is difficult to determine. Always follow the gauge stated in your pattern.

KNITTING NEEDLES															
U.S.	0	1	2	3	4	5	6	7	8	9	10	10½	11	13	15	17
U.K.	13	12	11	10	9	8	7	6	5	4	3	2	1	00	000	---
Metric - mm	2	2.25	2.75	3.25	3.5	3.75	4	4.5	5	5.5	6	6.5	8	9	10	12.75

◼◻◻◻ **BEGINNER**	Projects for first-time knitters using basic knit and purl stitches. Minimal shaping.
◼◼◻◻ **EASY**	Projects using basic stitches, repetitive stitch patterns, simple color changes, and simple shaping and finishing.
◼◼◼◻ **INTERMEDIATE**	Projects with a variety of stitches, such as basic cables and lace, simple intarsia, double-pointed needles and knitting in the round needle techniques, mid-level shaping and finishing.
◼◼◼◼ **EXPERIENCED**	Projects using advanced techniques and stitches, such as short rows, fair isle, more intricate intarsia, cables, lace patterns, and numerous color changes.

GAUGE

Exact gauge is **essential** for proper size. Before beginning your project, make a sample swatch in the yarn and needle specified. After completing the swatch, measure it, counting your stitches and rows carefully. If your swatch is larger or smaller than specified, **make another, changing needle size to get the correct gauge**. Keep trying until you find the size needles that will give you the specified gauge.

MARKERS

As a convenience to you, we have used markers to help distinguish the beginning of a pattern or the beginning of a round. Place markers as instructed. When you reach a marker on each row or round, slip it from the left needle to the right needle; remove it when no longer needed.

KNITTING IN THE ROUND

Using a circular needle, cast on all stitches as instructed. Untwist and straighten the stitches on the needle before beginning the first round. Place a marker after the last stitch to mark the beginning of a round. Hold the needle so that the skein of yarn is attached to the stitch closest to the right hand point.

To begin working in the round, knit the stitches on the left hand point (*Fig. 1*).

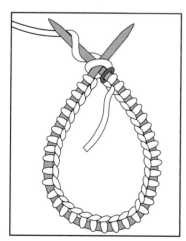

Fig. 1

Continue knitting around and around without turning the work; but for the first three rounds or so, check that the cast on edge has not twisted around the needle. If it has, it is impossible to untwist and must be ripped back to the cast on row.

When working on a project that is too small to use circular needles, double pointed needles are required. Divide the stitches into thirds or fourths and slip $1/3$ or $1/4$ of the stitches onto each of the double pointed needles (*Fig. 2*), forming a triangle or square and leaving the last needle of the set empty. With the last needle, knit across the first needle. You will now have an empty needle with which to knit the stitches from the next needle. Work the first stitch on each needle firmly to prevent gaps.

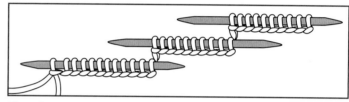

Fig. 2

DECREASES
KNIT 2 TOGETHER (abbreviated K2 tog)

Insert the right needle into the **front** of the first two stitches on the left needle as if to **knit** (*Fig. 3*), then **knit** them together as if they were one stitch.

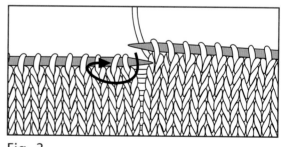

Fig. 3

KNIT 2 TOGETHER THROUGH BACK LOOP (abbreviated K2 tog tbl)

Insert the right needle into the **back** of the first two stitches on the left needle (*Fig. 4*), then **knit** them together as if they were one stitch.

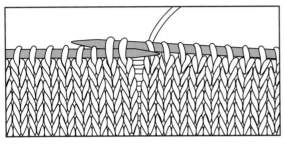

Fig. 4

SLIP, SLIP, KNIT (abbreviated SSK)

Separately slip two stitches as if to **knit** (*Fig. 5a*). Insert the **left** needle into the **front** of both slipped stitches (*Fig. 5b*) and knit them together (*Fig. 5c*) as if they were one stitch.

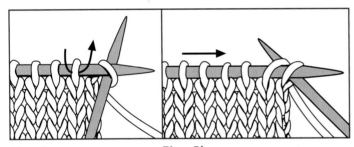

Fig. 5a   Fig. 5b

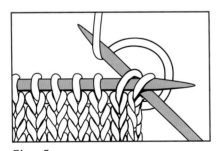

Fig. 5c

SLIP 1, KNIT 2 TOGETHER, PASS SLIPPED STITCH OVER
(abbreviated slip 1, K2 tog, PSSO)

Slip one stitch as if to **knit** (*Fig. 6a*), then knit the next two stitches together (*Fig. 3, page 73*). With the left needle, bring the slipped stitch over the stitch just made (*Fig. 6b*) and off the needle.

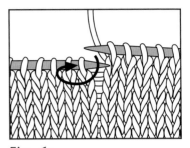

Fig. 6a

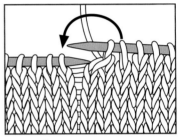

Fig. 6b

PURL 2 TOGETHER
(abbreviated P2 tog)

Insert the right needle into the **front** of the first two stitches on the left needle as if to **purl** (*Fig. 7*), then **purl** them together as if they were one stitch.

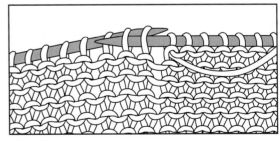

Fig. 7

PURL 2 TOGETHER THROUGH BACK LOOP (abbreviated P2 tog tbl)

Insert the right needle into the **back** of the first two stitches on the left needle as if to **purl** (*Fig. 8*), then **purl** them together as if they were one stitch.

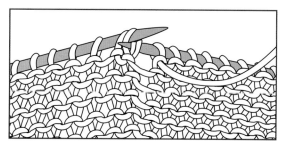

Fig. 8

INCREASES
KNIT INCREASE

Knit the next stitch but do **not** slip the old stitch off the left needle (*Fig. 9a*). Insert the right needle into the **back** loop of the **same** stitch and knit it (*Fig. 9b*), then slip the old stitch off the left needle.

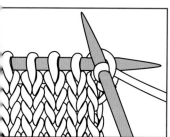 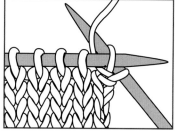

Fig. 9a   Fig. 9b

ADDING NEW STITCHES

Insert the right needle into stitch as if to **knit**, yarn over and pull loop through (*Fig. 10a*), insert the left needle into the loop just worked from **front** to **back** and slip the loop onto the left needle (*Fig. 10b*). Repeat for required number of stitches.

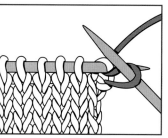 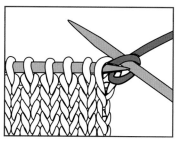

Fig. 10a   Fig. 10b

YARN OVERS
After a knit stitch, before a knit stitch

Bring the yarn forward **between** the needles, then back **over** the top of the right hand needle, so that it is now in position to knit the next stitch (*Fig. 11a*).

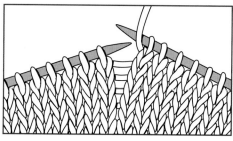

Fig. 11a

After a knit stitch, before a purl stitch

Bring yarn forward **between** the needles, then back **over** the top of the right hand needle and forward **between** the needles again, so that it is now in position to purl the next stitch (*Fig. 11b*).

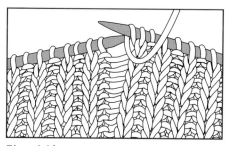

Fig. 11b

PICKING UP STITCHES

When instructed to pick up stitches, insert the needle from the **front** to the **back** under two strands at the edge of the worked piece (*Fig. 12*). Put the yarn around the needle as if to **knit**, then bring the needle with the yarn back through the stitch to the right side, resulting in a stitch on the needle. Repeat this along the edge, picking up the required number of stitches.

A crochet hook may be helpful to pull yarn through.

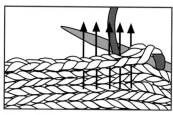

Fig. 12

STOCKINETTE GRAFTING

Insert a needle through the stitches of the Edging below the waste yarn/thread (*Fig. 13a*).

The threaded yarn needle should be on right side of work. Work in the following sequence, pulling yarn through as if to **knit** or as if to **purl** with even tension and keeping yarn under points of needles to avoid tangling and extra loops.

Step 1: Purl first stitch on **front** needle, leave the stitch on the needle (*Fig. 13b*).

Step 2: Knit first stitch on **back** needle, leave the stitch on the needle (*Fig. 13c*).

Step 3: Knit first stitch on **front** needle, slip the stitch off the needle (*Fig. 13d*).

Step 4: Purl next stitch on **front** needle, leave the stitch on the needle (*Fig. 13e*).

Step 5: Purl first stitch on **back** needle, slip the stitch off the needle (*Fig. 13f*).

Step 6: Knit next stitch on **back** needle, leave the stitch on the needle (*Fig. 13g*).

Repeat Steps 3-6 across until all stitches are worked off the needles, then carefully remove the waste yarn/thread.

Fig. 13a

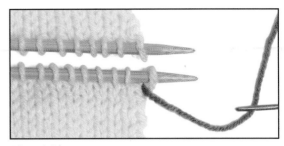

Fig. 13b

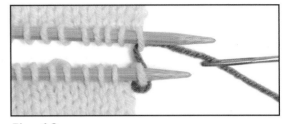

Fig. 13c

Fig. 13d

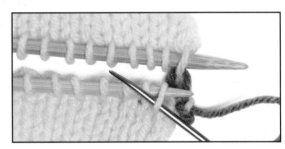

Fig. 13e

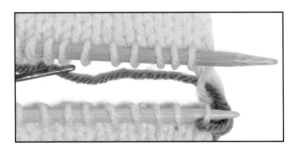

Fig. 13f

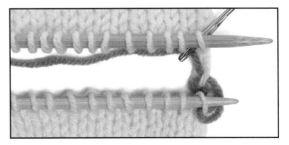

Fig. 13g